D1297351

Macedonio Fernández
and the Spanish American New Novel

The publication of this work has been made possible by assistance from the Center for Inter-American Relations, and the Andrew W. Mellon Foundation.

Macedonio Fernández and the Spanish American New Novel

Jo Anne Engelbert

A Center for Inter-American Relations Book

Published by
New York University Press. New York. 1978

Library of Congress Cataloging in Publication Data

Engelbert, Jo Anne.
   Macedonio Fernandez and the Spanish American new novel.

   Bibliography: p.
   Includes index.
   1. Fernández, Macedonio, 1874–1952—Criticism and
interpretation. I. Title.
PQ7797.F312Z63   863   77–76596
ISBN 0–8147–2153–2

Library of Congress Catalog Card Number: 77–76596.
ISBN: 0–8147–2153–2.

Manufactured in the United States of America.

To Walter

CONTENTS

CONTENTS

INTRODUCTION

"Theologians," said Borges in a speech on Macedonio Fernández, "say that each angel constitutes a separate species. Macedonio Fernández, himself a sort of angel, is of a lineage distinct from that of other men." On another occasion he said that "defining Macedonio" (for so he is affectionately called, without surname) "is like trying to define red in terms of another color".[1] As an artist he certainly seems to have been inspired by a mutant muse, for his poetry, fiction, humor, and metaphysics are as unclassifiable as the fauna of another planet. Macedonio is one of those writers who now and then appear in history out of chronological or any other sort of order, challenging existing categories for comparison and evaluation. His life and work present a series of paradoxes. Born in 1874, the same year as Leopoldo Lugones, Macedonio was in no way associated with the Modernist movement. A man who wrote incessantly and who believed in the transcendental powers of literature, Macedonio was usually indifferent

to publication, and the majority of his work would surely
have been lost had it not been for the dogged vigilance of
friends. A writer, if there ever was one, for *paucorum
hominem,* Macedonio astonishingly made Argentine best-
seller lists in 1967, with a new edition of *Papeles de Recienvenido (Newcomer's Papers).* Considered by many Argen-
tines a kind of symbol of *criollismo,* an indispensable
element of Argentinity like *mate,* the tango, and the *ombú,*
he never concerned himself with telluric or sociological
themes, never evoked the pampa or the gaucho, and
wrote in an idiom described by Juan Ramón Jiménez as a
kind of personal Esperanto.[2] Most paradoxical of all, his
posthumous novel, *Museo de la novela de la Eterna (Museum
of the Novel of Eterna),* seems to have engendered novels by
Cortázar, García Márquez, and Cabrera Infante, as one re-
viewer put it without these gentlemen ever having read it.[3]

Had it been published during Macedonio's lifetime,
Museo would certainly be recognized today as an indisputable progenitor of the Spanish American new novel. If it
had been published in 1940 instead of 1967, literary
manuals would now routinely list its innovations as clear
premonitions of the great experimental narratives of
recent years. All of the features we now associate with the
Spanish American new novel were present in *Museo*: the
assault upon Cartesian development, the rejection of
mimesis, the insistent metaphysical overtones, the aspiration to an autonomous, self-subsistent text, the role of the
reader as co-participant in the creation of the novel, the
open ending, and, above all, the self-contesting, experimental air of the entire enterprise. If instead of keeping his
manuscript in a chaotic heap beside his bed, accumulating
layers of tobacco, *yerba* and crumbled *alfajores,* Macedonio
had actually taken it to a printer, we could have ascribed
legitimate, *criollo* grandpaternity to works like *Hopscotch*

and *One Hundred Years of Solitude,* and graduate students could now devote endless hours to elaborating intricate chains of genetic relations. Instead, *Museo* was published in 1967, fifteen years after Macedonio's death, and it is not easy to link it to the works that came "after" it. We shall obviously have to dispense with conventional talk of influence, noting only that Macedonio's new novel was even newer than the new novels it might have inspired— "the most experimental book to date," according to Emir Rodriguez Monegal.[4]

Borges has observed that every writer creates his precursors by teaching us to read them with new eyes. The Spanish American new novelists have created a Macedonio who is simultaneously their splendid precursor and logical successor. Because of them, we can read Macedonio with a special delight and with a heightened awareness of what his assault upon Western literature really signifies. And because of Macedonio—who unwittingly carried the experiments of the new novelists to their logical extreme— the trajectory they initiated is further extended. *Museo* may very well be the book Cortázar's Morelli dreamed of writing, a post-Macondo text, the only kind of narrative still conceivable *after* the vaporization of Melquíades's fatidic parchments.

Macedonio's literary radicalism is an expression of his deep-seated disaffection from the culture in which he lived and worked, a disaffection not essentially ideological or political but metaphysical. What his novel challenges is nothing less than an entire world view, a whole system of assumptions concerning reality, time and the self. If *Museo* is more experimental than other new novels, this is because it contests not only the literary system of the Western world, but the principles of life and thought upon which this system rests. Macedonio's literary experiments, then, are never arbitrary, never intended merely to disconcert or to perplex, but are always the logical extension of the metaphysical speculation that was his passion. This being true, we cannot consider his narratives apart from his metaphysics.

We shall approach *Museo*, therefore, from Macedonio's book of metaphysical essays. *No toda es vigilia la de los ojos abiertos* (*Not All Waking Consciousness Is the Open-Eyed Variety*), which is the best possible introduction to his Idealism. The principal ideas of these essays will serve as a basis for understanding Macedonio's aesthetics and particularly his highly original theory of the novel. His narrative technique and his achievement as a novelist will be considered within this frame of reference.

In the growing collection of Macedoniana, nothing is more perplexing than the statements of knowledgeable commentators regarding the place of Macedonio Fernández in Spanish American literature. "The man who has had the greatest influence upon the significant literature of our times," wrote Ramón Gómez de la Serna in *Sur* in 1937; "Spiritual master of the writers of an entire era," according to Pagés Larraya; one of the four "founders of literary modernity in Spanish America," says Carlos Fuentes in *La nueva novela latinoamericana*. Canal Feijóo observes, "One thinks of him as the cornerstone of an entire literary tradition." "Maître de tous," writes H. A. Murena in *Les lettres nouvelles*.[5] We could lengthen indefinitely the list of references to Macedonio the spiritual master, the father, the founder, and cornerstone, with quotations from Alfonso Reyes, Borges, and others well qualified to comment, and yet add little to our understanding. For the urgent references to this important influence are without exception unspecified, undocumented. Nowhere in the foregoing citations do we find a specific mention of authors, works, and dates. Macedonio's influence is in fact a most elusive commodity. Borges, pressed by an interviewer to specify, responded with a tired, or amused "Does he have any influence?" (The same Borges who said in Macedonio's funeral address, "In those days I imitated him, to the extreme of transcription, to the extreme of devout and passionate plagiarism"?)

It must give us pause that the perceptive observers who have made these comments have not gone beyond their instinctive assertion of Macedonio's condition of spiritual master, originator, and founder. What happens when we analyze this influence so fervently affirmed? If we cannot specify it, or if it constantly eludes our grasp, what, if anything, can be its substance? Ought we to take it seriously? Considering the credentials of the witnesses, we should indeed, for this is hardly a case of literary mass hysteria. One difficulty is that we are dealing with a phenomenon that manifested itself largely through the medium of the spoken rather than the written word. Macedonio published little during his lifetime and in very limited editions. His principal contact with his disciples was conversation, and that evanescent substance must be seriously considered as among the chief products of his genius. His written words, according to one observer, are "the least interesting fraction of his literature." González Lanuza says that his published work, rich and profound as it is, is poor and pale in comparison to his converstation, his presence. Reconstructing Socratic colloquies of fifty years ago would seem to be an impossible task, but more than one of Macedonio's friends has attempted to transcribe fragments of the master's conversation in an affectionate profile or article. These few recorded idealist paradoxes, unorthodox opinions, and flashes of wit are all that now remains of Macedonio's conversation for those not privileged to have heard the man talk.

The chief difficulty, however, in specifying Macedonio's influence lies in the nature of the influence itself. Macedonio, rather than imparting any sort of doctrine, seemed to awaken native mental powers in each of those who heard him. "Macedonio taught one to think" is an observation we find again and again in the comments of those who knew him. "Author of authors," a phrase which Macedonio applied to Ramón Gómez de la Serna, perfectly describes Macedonio himself, according to poet Lizardo Zía. Zía, in a piece written in 1928, speaks of an emotional as well as intellectual response to Macedonio's conservation: "I feel a great confidence in myself when I am with him. I feel that everything will turn out well, and I have the courage to tackle anything." "Macedonio 'taught' Socratically, without didacticism; he was rather a gentle, patient *paterfamilias*," recalls an old friend, poet Ilka Krupkin. "An inspirer," concludes another close friend, poet and essayist Canal Feijóo.[6] Each man was touched, but each in his own way, experiencing not so much a desire to imitate the master as an awakening of the intuition, a discovery of unsuspected resources within himself.

"The great teachers were all oral teachers," said Borges, in a talk on Macedonio Fernández. "Pythagoras, Buddha and Christ left no written texts." This remarkable statement was not intended to negate Macedonio's written work, but rather to suggest that this work is only a partial revelation of the man. "Like all authentic teachers, he was superior to his work," Borges adds. "His teaching was oral in character and did not reside in his words but in his radiant presence."[7]

"The image which a writer leaves in others is also a part of his work," Borges says in his book on Lugones, and this observation is especially meaningful when applied to Macedonio. The image left in others by Macedonio Fernández (in contrast to Lugones) lingers on, more luminous than ever, decades after his death, affecting a generation who never knew him personally. For Macedonio has become "the center of an affectionate mythology." According to Pagés Larraya, Macedonio is at present one of two indisputable myths among students of literature at the University of Buenos Aires (the other being, not surprisingly, Roberto Arlt). *Macedonio* is the title of a current avant-garde literary magazine, and according to poet Rodolfo Alonso, Macedonio is one of the few idols of the generation of 1950, a highly regarded "symbol of the anti-literary."[8] The Macedonian mythology continues to be elaborated in dozens of nostalgic articles written by friends who recall his eccentricities, his phobias, and his tenderness, and who evoke some incident such as the presidential campaign or the novel–in–the–street because they share with Borges the desire that "nothing of Macedonio be lost." This legacy of reminiscence–becoming–myth, despite its subjectivity, is useful in the critical evaluation of his accomplishment, for it enlightens to some extent that area beyond the edges of the paper where he continued to exert his creative powers, leaving an indelible "image in others."

The enemy of mimesis did not believe in portraiture. A portrait, he believed, did not convey a *likeness* of a subject but merely a single moment of his individuality from which *nothing* should be inferred regarding his past or future natures; "the congruence of character is a senseless concept, as is the concept of the congruence of the Cosmos and of Reality as a whole" ("Inéditos de Macedonio,"

Hispamérica, 1:51). The holder of such radical theories of art and personality will induce a formidable methodological crisis in the souls of his future biographers. Certainly the traditional course of tracing "development," of searching in a welter of detail for the indispensable "keys" to life and work, ought to be dismissed as not only futile but decidedly anti-Macedonian. Although the genre of Macedonian biography has not as yet been invented, we have nevertheless included a considerable amount of biographical information in the first chapter; Macedonio is still relatively unknown outside of Argentina, and very few studies of his life and work are available in this country. The details assembled are intended to be seen as a kind of composite of "single moments" included for the sake of their intrinsic interest; their "congruence" or lack of it may be pondered indefinitely by the readers of the curious novelist-angel Macedonio Fernández.

I am deeply grateful to John Alexander Coleman, one of the first critics to perceive the full significance of Macedonio's radical experiments in the novel, for his invaluable critical insight and infinitely patient guidance. I am heavily indebted to Adolfo de Obieta for sharing unsparingly his privileged understanding of the spirit and letter of his father's work. My thanks also to Ilka Krupkin and Luis Soler Cañas for innumerable kindnesses and for the abundance of documents from their personal archives they so generously shared with me. I am especially appreciative of the support of the Center for Inter-American Relations in the publication of this book and of the warm encouragement of Ronald Christ. My research in Argentina was made possible by a study grant from the American Association of University Women.

All translations in the book are mine unless otherwise indicated.   J.E.

Abbreviations of Works
by Macedonio Fernández

M   *Museo de la novela de la Eterna* (*Museum of the Novel of Eterna*) (Buenos Aires: Centro Editor, 1967).

PR29   *Papeles de Recienvenido* (*Newcomer's Papers*) (Buenos Aires: Editorial Proa, 1929).

PR44   *Papeles de Recienvenido. Continuación de la nada.* (*Newcomer's Papers. Continuation of Nothing*) (Buenos Aires: Losada, 1944).

PR66   *Papeles de Recienvenido, poemas, relatos, cuentos, miscelánea* (*Newcomer's Papers, Poems, Stories, Tales, Miscellany*) (Buenos Aires: Centro Editor, 1966).

NTV   *No toda es vigilia la de los ojos abiertos* (*Not All Waking Consciousness Is the Open-Eyed Variety*) (Buenos Aires: Centro Editor, 1967).

Chapter I

The Long Gestation of a Novelist

Once it had floated into his consciousness, the idea of writing *La novela de la Eterna* claimed a gradually increasing share of Macedonio's attention; the never-ending novel became a kind of personal Zahir. As his interest in other genres dissolved with the years, his interest in the novel intensified. *La novela de la Eterna* would be the culmination of his aspirations both as thinker and as artist. As a metaphysician, Macedonio had discovered with Unamuno and Sartre that the novel has enormous potential for the awakening of philosophical insight. As an artist, he had a vision of a text so unorthodox that its realization would constitute a challenge to the most fundamental concept in the system of Western literature, the concept of the literary *work*. The radical text-in-the-making, as it is called by Noé Jitrik,[1] was conceived by Macedonio as an unending book, a novel being perpetually created, different for each new reader. Although

1

he worked on this text for several decades, Macedonio's death in 1952 interrupted his experiments without the novel's having reached a definitive, final version—if, indeed, it was ever intended to do so. The manuscript itself was a haze of visions and revisions, but with patience, skill, and scrupulous scholarship, these pages were eventually organized into a book by the poet Adolfo de Obieta,* Macedonio's son, editor, and daily companion during the last years of his life. The book, called *Museo de la novela de la Eterna* (*Museum of the novel of Eterna*), was published in 1967, some forty years after the writing of certain portions, In a sense, the novel was the work of a lifetime, for all that had gone before—the metaphysical ruminations, the aesthetic theories, the humor, the poetry, the fragmentary short stories—all became part of it.

The novel is not only open-ended, but indeed seems reluctant to relinquish its ideal existence by even beginning: fifty-six prologues gently introduce the reader into the mysterious world of la Eterna. Adolfo de Obieta, speculating about his father's intentions, remarks in his preface to *Museo*: "Perhaps he was just playing with the

*Macedonio lived with his son Adolfo de Obieta, from 1943 until his death in 1952. Distinguished poet and essayist in his own right, Adolfo de Obieta has taken upon himself the bewildering task of deciphering, transcribing, and preparing for publication the large number of manuscripts left by his father. He has edited new and greatly enlarged editions of *Papeles de Recienvenido* and *No toda es vigilia la de los ojos abiertos,* and in 1967 he completed the monumental task of assembling from his father's notes *Museo de la novela de la Eterna.* He is currently preparing for Ediciones Corregidor a ten-volume series of *Obras completas.* No literary executor has performed his critical task with more intelligence, or more love; Argentinians will long be grateful that the papers of one of their most original writers were given into such capable hands.

prologues, playing with the titles, playing with the novel —but in general he was very serious in the way he went about it; perhaps he played so long that another game, apparently of a higher order, eventually interrupted the author's game with his characters and his readers." In one of the prologues, seventy-three-year-old Macedonio wonders whether critics will describe him as a "promising novelist." "Promising novelist" was the final stage of a very long metamorphosis, a sporadic literary career spanning six decades in which Macedonio was variously journalist, humorist, essayist, poet, and short story writer. The novelist, of course, is prefigured in much of his early work. It is instructive to trace the course of his long preoccupation with the definition of the novel.

Macedonio Fernández wrote incessantly all the years of his long life. His peculiar calligraphy absentmindedly covered whatever surface was at hand—envelopes, bus tickets, margins, and napkins—in a continuous, automatic discharge of mental energy. Writing for him was coincidental with thinking, but thinking was primary; an editorial concern for the definitive exposition of his thought gripped him only sporadically. There is a remarkable integrity in every manifestation of his mind, every facet of his art, for he is not the detached "theorizer of his own works," as he has been called, but a tireless verifier of his own theories. His theories are, without exception, working hypotheses, live options to be acted upon. He is incapable of exploiting an ingenious notion of Hume or Berkeley for the sake of its aesthetic possibilities; the ideas that abound in his work are invariably ideas that are real and true for him. All his theories are ultimately related to a total metaphysical quest, a personal solution to the mystery of being. For this reason his life and work seem all of a piece: his conversation, an extension of his art; his art—

humor, poetry, and fiction—an extension of his meta-physics. As in Unamuno, genres all but disappear: story turns essay and essay becomes poem; poem trails into philosophical treatise and treatise turns novel, all genres being different modes of expressing the same essential concerns. The novel, however, ultimately occupied his full attention. Toward the end of his life, philosopher, humorist, poet, and narrator merged into a final incarnation: novelist of la Eterna.

Early Years

Macedonio begins two of his spurious autobiographies, a genre he was fond of, with the often-quoted statement. "The Universe or Reality and I were born on June 10, 1874, and it is simple to add that both births occurred near here in a city called Buenos Aires. There is a world for every birth, and there is nothing personal about not being born—it just means not happening to have a world (*Papeles de Recienvenido* [hereafter cited as PR 29], p. 9.)".[2]

Reality was to vanish with him on February 10, 1952. In the interim, he remained almost exclusively within the environs of Buenos Aires: except for a brief residence in Misiones and an occasional excursion to Uruguay or Paraguay, Macedonio rarely left the capital. His family counted ten generations born on American soil; his ancestors included conquistadors and colonists. His father, also improbably named Macedonio, was a wealthy *estanciero* and property holder. He died when Macedonio, the oldest son, was seventeen. For his mother, doña Rosa del Mazo, Macedonio had deep affection and an admiration that approached reverence. In his poem "My Mother, Vision of God" ("Dios visto, mi madre"), he pays loving tribute to her:

Eternal Mistress of the Three Verities:
Ethics, Mystic Vision, Practicality.
Clear-eyed being
In whom there was never
a doubt of Reality
    or of Conduct
a selfish impulse
a moment of fear
nor the least hestitation in Sacrifice
In whom there was never
a complaint
a tear
a superstition
nor the slightest displeasure
that anything should live
that anything should die
for in her there was never
a single thought
of herself.   (1929); *Papeles de
Recienvenido, poemas relatos, cuentos, miscelánea* [here-
after cited as PR 66], p. 258).

The six children from oldest to youngest were Gabriela,
Macedonio, Adolfo (important in the history of Argentine
socialism), Mariano, Arturo, and Eduardo, a somewhat
eccentric international target-pistol champion. Macedonio
attended the Colegio Nacional and the Law School of the
University of Buenos Aires. He received the degree of
Doctor of Jurisprudence in 1897. Unfortunately, his
dissertation, entitled "De las personas" ("On Persons"),
has been lost. Relatives recall that he scandalized university
authorities by requesting from the municipality a cer-
tificate of poverty so that he might be excused from
wearing formal attire at graduation exercises.

Macedonio must have begun to write when very young indeed. By his middle teens he had perfected a humorous style that combined the grace and sophistication of Larra with the wit and diction of Quevedo, both of whom he had obviously read with admiration. At seventeen, while still a university student, he published a series of delightful pieces in a newspaper called *El Progreso,* edited by a relative, Octavio de Acevedo.[2] The paper relied heavily on contributions by university students, and among selections by Macedonio's classmates we find poems by one Jorge Borges, father of Jorge Luis. In 1892 *El Progreso* published seven short articles by Macedonio. With the exception of "La revolución democrática," which is painfully earnest, all are short, humorous articles of the genre made popular by Larra, Nájera, and others. In "La calle Florida," for example, Macedonio, with a deftness hardly to be expected in a seventeen-year-old, gives us the following likeness of a fashionable young man:

He was supported by a tripod formed by his two legs and a stout cane, which did not always serve as a foot, since it was sometimes seen to whirl between the fingers of his upper extremities, giving him the appearance of a windmill.

This similarity brought to mind the extravagances of the immortal creation of Cervantes, and I could not help but think that should the Knight of the Sad Countenance have passed by in that instant, he would have given this individual his comeuppance.

The subject was more clothes than person. Both his hands and his feet were upholstered in black kid. The rest of his garments were of the same color, as was the cornice of the edifice, I should say his hat, so that the total impression of obscurity was that of a scholastic argument.

His nose upheld a pair of lenses positioned like shop windows in front of his eyes; from the spectacles there descended a chain which lost itself among the folds of his clothing; another chain emerged from a pocket of his waistcoat only to enter a neighboring pocket, and a third chain, of heavier links, burst forth from within his coat, so that he was a veritable explosion of chains, or if you will, a symbol of liberty. (*El Progreso,* September 25, 1892.)

As far as is known, Macedonio never again tried his hand at this kind of "costumbrista" writing. The type of humor that was to interest him in later years was conceptual rather than satirical, and its social content was purely incidental. What we ought to note perhaps is that these articles give evidence of a very early affinity with Quevedo, to whom Macedonio the humorist is often compared. In "La música" Macedonio speculates about the physical appearance of two neighbor ladies he calls "my tormentors" because of the piano-induced tortures they inflict upon him. In a baroque sentence or two he transforms them into sinister spinster-spinets:

They are probably as small in stature and as elegant in appearance as the instrument they use to torture me. I imagine their arms to be like the candelabra used to illumine the score, their fingers yellowish like the keys of old pianos, with nails the color of the black keys—in short, they are walking pianos. (*El Progreso* August 14, 1892.)

Macedonio's extensive readings in philosophy and the social sciences during the next few years affected him profoundly. It was a sober and pensive Macedonio who in 1896 published three articles in Carlos Vega Belgrano's admirable newspaper *El Tiempo*. Entitled "Psicología atomística," "La ciencia de la vida," and "El problema moral," the three articles contain serious reflections on human behavior and the nature of society, prompted for the most part by Macedonio's reading of Renan, Tarde, Guyau, Delboeuf, Ribot, Richet, Maury, Fouillée, and others. The essays are a curious mixture of physiology, psychology, atomic theory, and classical wisdom—a collage of observations culled from hundreds of sources, pieced together by an earnest young man who has set for himself the task of making sense of life.

The hope of reaching the ultimate "truth of things" had already gripped him, already kept him reading late into the night, scribbling reams of notes, writing to philosophers he admired. A letter received by Macedonio from the French philosopher Arréat has chanced to be preserved because Vega Belgrano found it interesting enough to publish. It gives us an idea of Macedonio's early philosophical preoccupations:

> Your first question seems to me a bit rash. Your are looking for an atomic substratum to correspond to the unity of the self. Well, if the atom is for you a material entity, you will have difficulty in expressing the self in mechanical or geometric terms; and if you think of it as a center of energy, how will you distinguish it, or why would you wish to separate it from the soul-substance whose ground it would be? We must take the facts as they are: on one hand we have a functional activity, complex in its manifestation; on

the other, a complex, whole, equally intricate, of cells, tissues, organs and body structures. In order to establish a correlation between the two, it would be necessary to know, beforehand, precisely that which is the object of your search, namely, the nature of the self. (*El Tiempo*, May 21, 1896, 150)

Arréat could not have been more correct. To understand the mystery of consciousness, to arrive at a satisfactory concept of the self, had become Macedonio's obsession. This preoccupation would lead him to consult, and ultimately reject, the works of most of the Western philosophers and psychologists who have considered the problem. His own meditations concerning the nature of the self, and certain insights arising, in all probability, out of his study of Schopenhauer, would carry him further and further away from the mainstream of Western philosophy. His continual wrestling with this question, not only on an intellectual plane, but as an emotional and spiritual concern, would have extremely important implications for his theory of art. It is interesting, therefore, to have the documentation of his early readings and meditations afforded by the *El Tiempo* articles. They make it clear that even as a very young man Macedonio was concerned with the question of the self, and that, as his readings indicate, he was gleaning ideas and information from every conceivable discipline. Not for some thirty years, however, until his long metaphysical essay, *No toda es vigilia la de los ojos abiertos* was published in 1928, would his most arresting insights be shared with any but his closest friends.

The home of doña Rosa del Mazo continued to be a meeting place for young intellectuals after the death of Macedonio's father. Juan B. Justo, José Ingenieros, Cosme

Mariño, Leopoldo Lugones, Julio Molina y Vedia, Carlos
Muscari, Jorge Borges, and Ignacio and Marcelo del Mazo
were frequent guests. Macedonio and his brother Adolfo
were an important part of their discussions. Juan B. Justo,
head of the Argentine socialist movement, was strongly
supported in his work by Adolfo, who, like Lugones and
Ingenieros, was actively engaged in working for the cause.
It is probable that the idea of establishing a Utopian colony
in Paraguay was first suggested by some member of this
tertulia. This experiment in Spencerian socialism was to
take place on an island belonging to the family of Molina
y Vedia. The date of the expedition may have been 1897,
perhaps earlier. The Utopians, all young men of wealthy
and socially prominent families, included Macedonio,
Arturo Muscari, Julio Molina y Vedia, and a group of their
friends. Nattily dressed in khaki, they set out in shiny boots
to establish in the jungles of Paraguay a socialist paradise.
The experiment seems to have perished even as it began,
possibly because of the counteractivity of jungle mos-
quitoes who had considered the paradise their own. The
dream of fraternity of kindred spirits did not perish,
however, and Macedonio cherished throughout his
lifetime the idea of achieving such a union. He realized the
dream literarily, at least, in the communual life of the
spirit depicted in *Museo de la novela de la Eterna*.

Macedonio's relationship to socialism is problematical.
His admiration of Juan B. Justo, his participation in the
experiment in Paraguay, and his contributing to the
inflammatory socialist organ *La Montana* have led some
commentators to hastily equate Macedonio's early interest
in socialism with that of his brother Adolfo, or with that
of Lugones or Ingenieros. In fact, in political science as in
other realms, Macedonio's opinions were heterodox and
utterly his own, never following expected, official lines.

The editors of *La Montaña,* had they paused to consider the implications of what Macedonio *said* in his sole contribution in May 1897 (Brumario, XXVI de la Comuna), might well have thought better of publishing it. Entitled "La desherencia," this brief essay gently ridicules the self-important pronouncements of nineteenth-century social prophets. Beside Ingenieros's fierce condemnation of the "reptiles burgueses" and Lugones's fiery incitements ("It is legitimate for any citizen to evade the law, to laugh at the constitution and to defend himself with lies when lies threaten to destroy him"), which appeared in the same issue, Macedonio's essay is, if anything, counterrevolutionary. What Macedonio objected to primarily was socialism's pretentions to have resolved with an economic system humanity's problems in every sphere:

> [The nineteenth century] thinks that it has based its predictions (its sciences) on a total understanding of the concept of causality: it believes that in classifying sciences as rational and experimental it has achieved a clear vision of things; it believes that it has defined and even solved the social problem with the invention of socialism,* which is really only an economic system; it believes that there is nothing to be learned about aesthetics, its psycho-physiological system being eternal, as the poems of Lombroso or Weissman about heredity or about the wonders of serotherapy are eternal, as the psychological novels of Tarde, or Ribot, or Wundt are eternal, or the psychism of Fouillée or

*I believe that socialism provides a very satisfactory answer to the economic aspect of the social problem, that is to say, to the immediate questions, but the problem contains many other imponderables [note in original].

Paulsen, etc., etc.; it has not the slightest doubt that
the next century will eagerly accept its enormous
bequest of books and laboratories.

"La desherencia" ("Disinheritance"), as its title implies,
is a sober, end-of-the-century reflection that the nineteenth
century, for all the rhetoric of its positivist idols, not only
had little to bequeath to the twentieth century, but could
seriously be said to have disinherited its progeny, having
destroyed its own spiritual patrimony and replaced it with
materialist cant. "The century which is to abolish inheritance will itself inherit hardly anything." Macedonio's
remarks in "La desherencia" are a reliable indication of the
direction in which his thought was to progress. He will
continue to be skeptical of scientific procedures simplis-
tically applied to the solution of human problems;
though deeply interested in psychology (as a gateway to
metaphysics), he will deplore its intrusion into literature
(the "psychological" novel will always be for him a source
of amusement, when not of horror), and he will continue
to think of the socialist movement as being ideally suited
to achieving certain limited, concrete economic goals in
Argentina.

Though Macedonio rarely treated political themes in his
work, politics interested him, and he was not hesitant to
air his views in conversation and in letters to his friends.
His maxim was: "maximum of individual, minimum of
state." His friend Enrique Fernández Latour recalls:

> I knew him to be a liberal in politics and a follower
> of the classics in economics, particularly of the
> English. He had a horror of giantism and of bureau-
> cratic red tape and the increasingly restrictive legis-
> lation curtailing the rights of the individual. He
> frequently protested against what he called "legal

regimentation," for it already seemed excessive to him, even in those days. He professed a couple of ideas which certain schools consider reactionary. He believed in the inevitability of social and economic hierarchies (which saved his having to approve of them) and he defended capital, property, and the right of children to inherit their parents' wealth with genuine good faith. Government despoilment of inheritance seemed to him to be an irritating attack upon the principle of equality of opportunity, for he maintained that the manner in which the children of the rich are raised and educated is so much a part of them that depriving them of this constitutes a disability no less real than a physical amputation. Hence his aristocratism, a constant surprise to those who discovered it, an occasional source of friction . . . . (*La Nación,* February 5, 1956).

Macedonio, in politics as elsewhere, consistently eludes the convenient pigeonhole and asserts his indefatigable individuality.

"Attorney and Property Owner"
On New Year's Day 1901, an enraptured Macedonio wrote a poem:

Supplication to Life
Luminous tide of Life,
ebb and flow of being,
swelling now
with sighs of joy or pain
the bosom of a dawning century,
you have lifted our frail hearts
to the crest of a dream
about to break for us
against a shore unknown.

Take from us, if you will,
all chalices save one:
the brimming cup of love
be all our dole.
Let our two hearts,
lulled by the rhythmic lie of time,
forever dream as one,
borne by a single dream
to the shore of a single sigh.
                                    Amen.
                              (PR66, p. 245)

The poem was dedicated to Elena de Obieta, and the "supplication to life" was apparently granted: that same year Macedonio married Elena, in one of the most significant acts of his life. For the world Elena died in 1920, but for Macedonio, who had written "I do not believe in the death of those who love nor in the life of those who do not," she never ceased to be the luminous central figure of his meditations and his art. Elena de Obieta was a beautiful, intelligent, and sensitive woman, an exemplary wife and mother, tolerant of her husband's lack of practical sense, his addiction to interminable philosophical discussions, his outrageous jokes. She bore him four children, Macedonio, Elena, Adolfo, and Jorge. Until his wife's sudden illness and death in 1920, Macedonio seems to have lived a life conventional in every respect. In 1904 we find him listed in Hogg's *Guía biográfica,* a kind of *Who's Who* of the capital's affluent citizens:

Macedonio Fernández: Attorney and property owner, born in Buenos Aires in 1874, son of Macedonio Fernández, Argentine rancher, and doña Rosa del Mazo de Fernández, married to Elena O. de

Fernández, educated in the Colegio Nacional and Facultad de Derecho, member of the Gymnastic and Fencing Club. Bartolomé Mitre, 2120.[3]

Macedonio Fernández practiced law, "my pleasant profession," without much enthusiasm, for approximately twenty-five years. Sometime after 1910 he accepted the post of district attorney in Posada, Misiones. León Naboulet in his book *La justicia en Misiones* described his activity there as follows:

> The state attorney, Dr. Macedonio Fernández, one hundred times better prepared than the other representatives of Themis to be found in Misiones, and a man whose integrity was a permanent safeguard to the inhabitants of the region he had jurisdiction over, was fatally bitten by the serpent (I am referring to internal political intrigues) and was obliged to return to Buenos Aires. We at the front lines launched an attack—as open as a slap in the face—against Judge González, in defense of our friend Fernández, who really deserved better treatment. . . .[4]

The often-repeated story that Macedonio was dismissed from his post for refusing to sentence anyone is probably apocryphal. While in keeping with the extraordinary gentleness of his nature, the story would seem to be simply another fable in the "affectionate mythology" we have referred to. For one thing, it was not his duty to sentence criminals; he was not a judge, but a state attorney. For another, Macedonio had a strong sense of social responsibility (as evidenced, for example, by his serious essays on ethics in *El Tiempo*) which could hardly have permitted him to indulge his own romantic sentiments at the expense

B

of those persons his duty it was to protect. Moreover, Naboulet's statement makes it clear that Macedonio's dismissal was the result of petty political intrigue within the system, and this seems a perfectly reasonable explanation.

While in Posadas, Macedonio was named director of the library and earned a reputation as a man of letters. He met in this wilderness another alien of sorts, Horacio Quiroga. We can only imagine what must have been a fascinating encounter for both *raros* in that wild and remote region. Of their conversation only a fragment remains, recorded by Quiroga in a long letter to Lugones dated October 7, 1912:

> Macedonio Fernández, the state attorney, is a quasi man of letters. The first time I met him he took me aback with his opinion of Rodó: "His whole work is nothing but a page out of Emerson."
> So you see, Lugones, that even the legal profession has its rare phenomena.

Indeed. Quiroga makes no further comment.

Emir Rodríguez Monegal, who records the incident in *El desterrado*, observes:

> With the perspective of time it seems even stranger that Quiroga and Macedonio Fernández should have passed each other by without becoming acquainted, without recognizing one another, like two express trains whose paths cross at a little station lost in the jungle. Fifteen years later they were to meet again in Buenos Aires, but on opposite sides of the literary barricade: Quiroga, already famous, was about to be

shelved, even openly ridiculed, by the same generation of young Ultraists who would deify Macedonio, guildmaster of the new lyricism. The "quasi man of letters" was to become a model for the young writers, while Quiroga (and Lugones himself) were put into storage as figures of the past. . . . The history of literature is full of these paradoxes.[5]

Little is known of Macedonio's literary activity during the period between 1900 and 1920. He was writing poetry, almost certainly, but very few poems of this period ever appeared in print. Two remarkable short poems, however, "Suave encantamiento" ("Soft Enchantment") and "Tarde" ("Afternoon") were published in 1904 in the magazine *Martín Fierro,* directed by Alberto Ghiraldo. Twenty years later, Evar Méndez, director of the second *Martín Fierro,* reprinted the delicate "Suave encantamiento"* with the following note:

*SOFT ENCHANTMENT

Fathomless and full
as two brief, graceful immensities,
your eyes inhabit your countenance
like lords;
and when from their depths
I see
dallying and rising
the flame of a radiant soul,
it seems that the morning is arising from sleep,
shining, over there between sea and sky,
where that drowsy line rocks
between two blue empires,
the line where our hearts pause
to caress it with hopes,
to kiss it with their glance;

Was Macedonio Fernández a precursor of Ul-
traism? Twenty years ago, during an era which
admired brilliant, noisily eloquent poetry, Macedonio
Fernández published the compositions "Tarde" and
"Suave Encantamiento" in Alberto Ghiraldo's *Martín
Fierro*. We reprint the latter, which might be con-
sidered an anticipation of Borges, González Lanuza,
Nora Lange, Francisco Piñero, our Ultraists.

Free verse, disdainful of rhyme and conventional
rhythm, but highly euphonic. A pure, recondite
poetry of mysterious accent. An almost total lack of
punctuation, another characteristic of our new poetry.
But above all, a love of the kind of image particularly
prized by the Ultraists. Here is the poem, which was
published November 14, 1904, and which closes with
two admirable lines of the type which leave us in a
long reverie. (*Martín Fierro*, January 24, 1925)

Having at this time almost no contact with the official
literary world, the world of manifestos, movements, and
magazines, Macedonio was nevertheless quietly elaborating his own aesthetic revolution.

---

when our being meditates,
drying its tears,
and, silently,
throws itself open to all the breezes of Life;
when we glimpse
the ashes of days gone by
floating in the Past
like the dust of all our pilgrimages
left behind at the last turn of the road:
Eyes that open like mornings
and, closing, let evening fall.

(Translated by Paula Speck;
PR 66, p. 246).

Meditations.

"He lived to think, to a greater extent than any other man I have ever known," Borges tells us in the prologue to his anthology *Macedonio Fernández.* "I am thinking all the time, and I wish to think," Macedonio wrote to his Aunt Angela in 1905; "I want to know whether the reality which surrounds us has a key that can explain it or whether it is totally and definitively impenetrable." In a rare moment of self-revelation, Macedonio once described to a reporter the origins of his long struggle with the enigmas of existence:

> At the age of seventeen I entered a period of my life filled with anguish. For ten long years I suffered in silence, all alone in the face of the reality of things, abandoned in a desolate world that held no answers. Tormented by doubt, I fought desperately to find my way out of the sunless labyrinth which my life had become. But all I found was the anguish of my own solitude, impassive and eternal. . . . Since then I have lived alone with my own thought: thought which is disobedient and ill-controlled and which continues to be the only vice of my comfortless life. (Interview with César Porcio, *La Nación,* January 26, 1930).

The emphatic diction is undoubtedly the reporter's and not Macedonio's, but the statement does reveal that the habit of constant philosophical rumination was acquired when Macedonio was very young. The period beginning when Macedonio was seventeen was, of course, the period immediately following his father's death. "Ten long years of silent suffering" ended with his marriage to Elena, but with her death twenty years later he again encountered "the anguish of solitude, impassive and eternal."

Macedonio was convinced that the discipline most akin

to metaphysics, the science most likely to provide the kind of revelation he was seeking, was psychology. He read extensively on the subject and told Cêsar Porcio in the same interview that "The study of psychology has been the source of the greatest satisfactions of my life." As early as 1902 Macedonio wrote a letter to José Ingenieros, director of the journal *Archivos de Criminología*, proposing "the advantages of taking a spiritual approach to the study of the spirit, of attempting a 'psychological psychology,' if I may call it that, not bound by the limitations of physiological data. . . ." This brief letter is sufficient to indicate Macedonio's orientation, which was in sharp contrast to prevailing positivist attitudes in Argentina. His advocacy of a "psychological psychology" shows him to be once again several decades ahead of his time in his thinking.

Macedonio was an early and passionate admirer of William James. In the next chapter we shall examine the aspects of James's work that interested him, for at first glance it might seem that James's radical empiricism could have little appeal for a *místico-idealista,* as Macedonio called himself. The famous epistolary friendship between the two thinkers began in 1905. Asked how the correspondence began, Macedonio told Cêsar Porcio:

One night when my cerebral "Self" had fallen completely asleep, my subconscious provided me with the strand which eventually led to a great discovery. Afterwards, when I awoke from a long dream, I could not specify with any precision whether the images with which my subconscious had occupied itself were auditive or visual. I did not know and I am still unable to say whether I had dreamed about a page of a novel or about Wagner's *Die Meistersinger.*

This demonstrated that there were no "pure sensory states" as William James and the majority of the psychologists of that day insisted, but instead, simple references to the organs of perception. In a word, I had proved that sensations do not have "specificity." . . . In a long letter I explained my discovery and my conclusions to the great American psychologist. He wrote back telling me to keep trying to perceive the variety of the sensations by prolonging their perception in the sensory organs. I did this, but in spite of having been able to distinguish with complete clarity the affective states of dream, I have never yet been able to say precisely whether those states were auditive or visual. (*La Nación,* January 26, 1930.)

The correspondence between Macedonio and James continued from 1905 until 1911, the year of James's death. Of James's letters to Macedonio, only one seems to have been preserved, a fragment of which is quoted at the beginning of *No toda es vigilia la de los ojos abiertos.* No trace has been found of the certainly fascinating letters Macedonio addressed to James. A photograph of William James accompanied Macedonio wherever he went to live, occupying a place of honor beside his bed. Copies of James's books that Macedonio was especially fond of, *The Principles of Psychology* and the *Pluralistic Universe,* have notations in the margins indicating that he read and reread these works, apparently finding them a constant source of stimulation.

Macedonio began to write essays on metaphysical themes during his years as a practicing attorney and family man, that is, before Elena's death in 1920. Several essays, including "La metafísica" and "Bases en metafísica," both dated 1908, were included by Adolfo de

Obieta in the 1967 edition of *No toda es vigilia la de los ojos abiertos*. These early essays are helpful in tracing the evolution of Macedonio's thought as he moved further and further away from contemporary European philosophy, gradually elaborating a metaphysics he would call *"Mi Idealismo Absoluto."*

In 1920 Elena de Obieta died following abdominal surgery. It could be held that Macedonio never completely recovered from the shock of being separated from her, never reconciled himself to her death. To all outward appearances his reaction was certainly one of withdrawal from the world. He gave up the family home, asked relatives to take charge of the four children, and abandoned his profession forever. Fot the next twenty-five years he lived alone in dingy hotels and furnished rooms, his possessions reduced to a bed, a chair, a guitar, and a frying pan, his contact with his children limited to occasional weekend visits. A psychologist judging from external evidence alone might interpret these images of abandonment and renunciation as expressing the behaviour of a man crippled by unresolved grief. A perceptive priest might find a revelation of quite another order; Macedonio's renunciation of the world, his physical withdrawal from it, may not have been so much an emotional regression as a kind of spiritual evolution.

Macedonio's religiosity was as profound as it was unorthodox. He rejected conventional religious terminology and very rarely employed the word "Dios." "Religiosity is the perception of the liberty of the soul with respect to matter," he wrote. The soul was eternal and its freedom, sacred, but to name and define the mystery was to reduce it to human terms, to limit and thus diminish it, something man ought not to do. "I do not have your Faith," he wrote to his Aunt Angela in 1905, "but I

believe that the spark which animates us is indestructible;
I do not know whether or not a God exists and I cannot
believe that blessings and punishments are meted out, but
I firmly believe that the spark which burns in us cannot
be extinguished."

In one of the many poems inspired by the death of
Elena de Obieta, "Palabras terminan" ("Beyond Words"),
Macedonio wrote:

> Death,
> we went with her
> beyond your realm.
> Now we are back from Death.
> And now I am alone;
> she has turned her face toward you,
> but she is waiting for me.
> To name the Mystery is to make it vanish;
> neither Deity nor Heaven
> have named it:
> we have Mystery
> and neither Deity nor Heaven
> intervenes;
> Only the undiminished
> Whole-Mystery
> is eternal.
> We disdain the distraction of legends.
> Ours the Mystery
> without Name
> without Moment
> without Place.
>
> (1922; PR66, p. 255).

A certain Macedonio Fernández was destroyed by the
death of Elena de Obieta: Dr. Macedonio Fernández,

attorney, family man, member of the Gymnastic and
Fencing Club, the perhaps fictitious Dr. Fernández of the
Guía biográfica who existed socially for a time in this form,
possibly solely for the sake of Elena de Obieta. This guise
became superflous when she departed, and another
Macedonio emerged who, perhaps also for the sake of
being near her, lived out his remaining life in Carthusian
simplicity, his contact with the world reduced to a minimum, his hours of meditation the most meaningful of his
life. "I would like to spend my remaining days as a
mystic," he wrote to Gómez de la Serna in 1928.

Elena Bellamuerte.

Shortly after the death of Elena, Macedonio sat one day
in the office of his friend, attorney Guillermo Palacios
Hardy, and wrote a poem now considered his masterpiece,
"Elena Bellamuerte." For certain writers—Cortázar,
for example—writing is "a graphic record of a spiritual
progress." For Cortázar's character, the writer Morelli,
writing is the making of a *mandala*. Macedonio is a writer
of this genus: "I write . . . in order to preserve for my
future self some signs for evocation," he says, and there is
evidence that he meant this quite literally, that certain
symbols he set down on paper were primarily for himself.
The fate of "Elena Bellamuerte" bears this out. A poem
"so perfect that by itself it could justify a country or a
culture," in the words of poet Roy Bartholomew (*Cien
poesías rioplatenses,* p. 271), "Elena Bellamuerte" was very
nearly lost; having written it, having marked this moment
of spiritual significance, Macedonio hid the poem away and
forgot about it. He put the poem in a biscuit tin, which
remained in some closet in Hardy's study until Hardy's
death twenty years later. "What disconcerting evidence
that the text was not destined for publication, that it was

written as a necessary step in the process of his own spiritual reordering and progression, . . ." observes Bartholomew. In 1926, pressed by Hidalgo, Huidobro, and Borges to contribute a selection for their anthology *Indice de la nueva poesía americana,* Macedonio wrote a composition entitled "Elena Bellamuerte" which bears some relation to the original poem but is inferior to it poetically. When the original version was discovered in 1940, Adolfo de Obieta sent it to *Sur*, which published it in January 1941.

"Elena Bellamuerte" is a melody in an unaccustomed mode. The elegiac tone is perfectly sustained: it is the voice of one speaking beside a tomb with a sense of already shared eternity. But the mourner speaks a language to his beloved unlike the common tongues of men. Juan Ramón Jiménez, referring to this strangeness of diction, observes:

> Paradise is a place with neither space nor time, where everything is nowhere. . . . And in this nowhere, of Dante, for example, or Blake, or Hölderin, with his language of no place, is Macedonio Fernández.[6]

But the strangeness of the poem lies not only in its idiom but in the elusiveness of its ideas. We are in the presence of a poet whose concept of death is unfamiliar to us. "Death is fictitious," Macedonio wrote to his friend Ricardo Victorica,

> because being born is fictitious, as are the unity of the self, the unity and continuity of personal history, the unity and identity of the World, order in sorrow and in consciousness. Let us perceive ourselves, but let us

perceive ourselves as independent, as living from instant to instant, with a psyche and in a world of Total-Possibility; in this way all that there ever was for us and of us will come back to us, just as long as we exercise the state of mystical consciousness, without identity and without history.[7]

Neither a classical threnody nor a Christian elegy, but a vision of a luminous "partir sin muerte," "Elena Bella-muerte" is not a lament but a cluster of personal "signos de evocación":

Death is Beauty.
But an eager death,
a deathless departure at the dawn of a new day,
is Divinity.

Prospero.

The year after Elena de Obieta died, Jorge Luis Borges returned to Buenos Aires after seven years in Europe. He recalls his return as "a great spiritual adventure because of the discoveries of landscapes and of souls." Central among the personalities discovered or rediscovered at this moment was Macedonio Fernández:

Perhaps the major event of my return was Mace-donio Fernández. Of all the people I have met in my life—and I have met some quite remarkable men—no one has ever made so deep and so lasting an impression on me as Macedonio. A tiny figure in a black bowler hat, he was waiting for us on the Dársena Norte when we landed, and I came to inherit his friendship from my father. ("Autobiographical Notes," p. 64).

Thirty years later, speaking beside Macedonio's tomb, Borges again recalled this moment in his life:

> Argentina seemed to me an insipid place, no longer a land of picturesque barbarity and not yet a seat of culture; but I talked a couple of times with Macedonio and I understood that this gray man, who in a mediocre boarding house near Tribunales was discovering the eternal problems as if he were Thales of Miletus or Parmenides, could infinitely replace the centuries and the kingdoms of Europe. I spent my days reading Mauthner or elaborating the arid, stingy poems of the Ultraist sect—the Ultraist error; the knowledge that on Saturday in some sweet shop in El Once we would hear Macedonio explain the nonentity or the illusion of the self was sufficient, I remember very well, to justify my weeks. (Funeral address, pp. 145–47).

The discovery of Macedonio by Borges and his contemporaries coincides precisely with the dawn of the Ultraist movement in Argentina. Silver-haired, nearly fifty years old, an astonished Macedonio found himself somehow playing Prospero to a group of beardless, brilliant, and often incorrigible spirits, Argentina's ultraístas. His exact relation to each of the young writers in this group, the extent of his influence upon them, and the legitimacy of his denomination as precursor of Ultraism in Argentina are questions beyond the scope of this study, but this much is apparent: there was an immediate and intense affinity between these young poets and old-young Macedonio, an affinity that caused them to enthusiastically claim him as their own. Rodríguez Monegal observes,

Upon discovering him, the Ultraist clan realized the ambition of every revolutionary group with a sense of pride: the discovery of a precursor, the rapid invention of a genealogy. In his love for everything Argentine, in his antirhetoric (or neorhetoric), in his way of savoring a metaphor, in his pursuit of the metaphysical paradox, Macedonio Fernández seemed to have anticipated the Ultraists who were currently throwing to the winds the last vestiges of Modernism, scandalizing the bureaucratic epigones. Macedonio turned out to be a witness who had weathered the Modernist epic without ever being touched by it and who in long silence had elaborated the tools for its complete destruction. ("Macedonio Fernández," p. 171).

Evar Méndez provided the documentation necessary for claiming Macedonio a literary as well as spiritual precursor of the new generation when he published in *Martín Fierro* in 1925 Macedonio's "Soft Enchantment" (1904). His note, quoted earlier, refers to "Soft Enchantment" as "a possible anticipation of Borges, González Lanuza, Nora Lange, Francisco Piñero, our Ultraists."

Like Güiraldes, Macedonio allowed his name to be linked to the movement, although both men belonged chronologically to an earlier generation. It is ironic that the generation that made Macedonio its guru ("*semidiós acriollado,*" in the words of Petit de Murat) devoted much of its energy to the excoriation of writers like Lugones who were his exact contemporaries (Quiroga, who was taken to task, was actually four years *younger* than Macedonio, as Rodríguez Monegal notes in *El desterrado*.) Gómez de la Serna recalls his remark,

Because of the young artists of Buenos Aires, whom I met four years ago, I find myself totally absorbed in the problem of aesthetic theory. When I met them, they despoiled me with such prolixity, took from me such enormous bounty of outdated aesthetics that until now I have been unable to recoup my treasures of ignorance. . . . (*Sur*, 7:79).

Macedonio had much to give his devotees, and he denied them nothing. Throughout his life he was a generous encourager of the young. Always available to listen to a new draft of a poem or a different ending for a short story, or to discuss some point of aesthetics or metaphysics, on occasion he even provided funds from his own pocket for a private edition of the poems of a promising unknown poet. For Macedonio's own career as a writer, his contact with young men like Jorge Luis Borges, Eduardo González Lanuza, Raúl Scalabrini Ortiz, Leopoldo Marechal, Francisco Luis Bernárdez, Alberto Hidalgo, and others was critical. Without their constant efforts to have him set his ideas down in publishable form, to wrest manuscripts from him and get them into print, it seems likely that much of his own work would never have been brought to light.

For some, the history, as opposed to the prehistory, of Macedonio Fernández begins with a flash of humor that suddenly illumined the dessert course of the Figari banquet in 1924: a toast to Dr. Pedro Figari composed by Macedonio and entitled "La oratoria del hombre confuso" ("The Oratory of a Confused Man"), later published in Evar Méndez's *Martín Fierro*. Macedonio, who was acquainted with neither Dr. Figari nor his paintings, was somehow persuaded to attend the banquet by friends from *Proa* and *Martín Fierro* who had organized it in honor of the distinguished Uruguayan. At some time during the meal, Macedonio, who did not like to read aloud in public, slipped some crumpled handwritten sheets into the hand of his friend Enrique Fernández Latour and asked him to read them as a toast to the guest of honor. There has never been a toast quite like it. The banqueters, whirled through a mind-blowing conceptual funny-house, ached with laughter. Fernández Latour recalls,

This was his introduction, the man, by his own definition, "of confused oratory," and if on this occasion he convulsed an audience unprepared for his humor (I shall never forget the enormous eyes of Ricardo Güiraldes), he continued to convulse and to delight succeeding audiences who were not only prepared for his wit but eagerly awaited it. (*Sur*, Nos. 209–10:148)

Macedonio's long anonymity had definitely ended.

Recienvenido, Macedonio, and Borges.

Magazines combative, satirical, and lyrical bloomed in profusion at this moment, for they were the *sine qua non* of the activity of the new generation. "All these publications reflect the golden age of cliques and coteries, manifestos, little gazettes, literary baptisms and funerals; they are the common denominator of the generation."[8] A new sensibility was rapidly emerging, preparing to take up arms "against the hippopotamic impermeability of the 'honourable public,' against the funeral solemnity of the historian and the professor, which mummifies everything

it touches," in the words of Oliverio Girondo's "Mani-
fiesto de *Martín Fierro*." The humor of Macedonio Fernández was judged a formidable arm for piercing hippopotamic hide, and Macedonio was soon being persuaded to
collaborate on a number of avant-garde periodicals.

The first *Proa*, "Revista de renovación literaria," was
founded in 1922. Borges and Macedonio were prime
movers in the project, and it was in *Proa* that Macedonio
"began to shine," as Borges puts it, with the publication
of some humorous pieces, his first publications since 1904.
In *Las revistas literarias argentinas* we read,

> *Proa* was favored by two notable circumstances:
> first, the consolidation of the Ultraist movement;
> second, the appearance of Macedonio Fernández.
> This singular figure ("The only genius to shine in the
> entire history of Argentine intelligence," according
> to Alberto Hidalgo), . . . must have been about fifty
> at the time and was practically unknown in the
> literary world. . . . Macedonio Fernández was a dog-
> ged fervorizer of enthusiasms: to a great extent the
> transcendent Borges is his creation (Borges himself has
> said as much). And in the first *Proa*—which ought to
> be known as the *Proa* of Macedonio Fernández—
> his influence is well known. (p. 86)

One of the many delights to be found in the three issues
of this *Proa* is a curious review by Borges of a nonexistent
book by Macedonio Fernández. The book, to be sure,
was to appear eventually, but not for some six years, and
at the time Borges wrote the article, it could hardly have
consisted of more than two dozen sheets of foolscap. But
these were enough to convince Borges that Macedonio had
discovered a style of narration that was spontaneity
itself. The review reads as follows:

Macedonio Fernández: *El Recienvenido* [*"The New-comer"*].

Someone has equated, not unhappily, the theological act of creation with the art of writing, which augments universal reality with its verbal realities. In both cases we are dealing with a kind of hallucination, for we may think of living as a painful fable with which God entrances his own mind, multiplying himself in souls. Schopenhauer, in an eminent metaphor, has already compared the deity and the poet, pointing out that the small illusion of art is epitomized by the universal illusion of the theater within the theater which we see in Hamlet.

What interests me today are the stratagems by which life can be made novelesque. In the complex kind of plotting practised by Wells and company, following the tradition of Poe, the quotidianity of life is exact, and hallucination is achieved by introducing some absurd contingency which, reeled in later with the inflexible precision of a formula, is sufficient to topple the previously rigid edifice. The same could be said about Swift: in his chimerical satires, however astonishing, there is never more than a single instant of strong imaginative activity: one single detour which turns the course of the work toward a marvellous channel. There are other scriveners who attempt to achieve the fantastic by packing in demons, succubi, and witches' sabbaths. All that can be said about them is that they are parasitic upon the imaginations of others and that they are shamefully dependent upon the tricks of time. Quevedo, in the episodes with which he begins his *Hora de todos,* seems to achieve a kind of continuous and uninhibited creation, but little by little the reader becomes aware of a stockroom full of Stoic moralizing and the book which began as pure mischief ends with solemn set-pieces and attacks upon the government. As for Gómez de la Serna, all he does is report on life with maniacal insistence on detail. His excellence is rooted in his style, not in his vision, which is oppressive, opaque, and carnal.

Generalizing from the previous examples, I should like to suggest that the imaginative novel is nothing more than the doggedly logical exploitation of a single whim. I know of only one exception. *In the digressions of Macedonio Fernández I seem to see an imagination in constant exercise: an activity which buoyantly goes on designing universes, not codified and fatal like a chess problem, but impromptu and mischievous like a good game of truco.** In order to fully appreciate him, it is sufficient to enjoy a well-defined, matchless, and distinctive individuality, like yours—oh reader! —you, who like everyone, exercise the plausible singularity of being someone. J. L. B. [emphasis added] (*Proa* [July 1923])

Written in the style Borges winces to recall, the review of *El Recienvenido,* the reader will have noticed, contains only one specific mention of Macedonio Fernández, but it is an important one. Borges seems to have realized even before Macedonio the implications of certain of his humorous techniques for the craft of storytelling. The

---

*An Argentine card game that requires the player to give quick, intuitive responses to very rapid accidents of play. [author's note]

possibility of a narrative spun by "*una fantasía en incesante ejercicio*" was understandably fascinating to the future author of "Tlön, Uqbar, Orbis Tertius."

The pseudonym chosen by Macedonio, "Recienvenido" (Newcomer to the literary world), was soon familiar, for the energy and humor of Macedonio's lines were a fine counterpoise to the self-conscious artiness of *Proa*. His irony, his irreverence, and the vigor of his prose are as notable in *Proa* as the smell of a good cigar in a tearoom full of ladies.

Macedonio's presence in *Proa* manifests itself when least expected, frequently summoned by the pen of Borges. In Borges's study of the poetry of Maples Arce, for example, we read,

> And since we are speaking of images, I should like to point out to those interested in studying them that point out to those interested in studying them that there are dozens of mutilated or aphonic comparisons hidden in our daily speech, whose pithiness goes completely unnoticed. To remark that the word "alero" [eave] derives from "ala" [wing] is an etymological commonplace; but to write, as Macedonio Fernández writes: "The eave shelters the house as a wing shelters a nest of baby birds . . ." is to restore new life to an old surprise and to restore to the language an accurate metaphor. (*Proa*, first cycle, 1.)

The first *Proa*, with its "three pages which unfolded like the kind of mirror which makes mobile and varied the immobile grace of the woman it reflects," as Borges nostalgically recalls, lasted for only three issues. Certainly one of its major accomplishments was the official introduction of Macedonio Fernández, "Recienvenido," to the literary world.

The second *Proa* (1924–26) saw the culmination of Ultraism. Directed by Jorge Luis Borges, Alfredo Brandán Caraffa, Ricardo Güiraldes, and Pablo Rojas Paz, the second *Proa* proposed to be a kind of instrument of consolidation in a garden of bifurcating aesthetic creeds. Another of its aims, interestingly enough, was to bridge the literary generation gap: "One ancient, fecund warrior is worth more to our cause than ten negative, frivolous youths." The fecund, ancient warrior chosen to act as guide and numen was, not surprisingly, Macedonio Fernández.

In the second *Proa* Macedonio revealed yet another facet of his genius. The September 1924 issue carried the first of Macedonio's metaphysical essays to appear in print. Macedonio had shared with his circle of disciples many of his ideas. We have only to look at such essays as Borges's curious "La nadería de la personalidad" ("The Nothingness of Personality") with its five dense paragraphs beginning, "The self does not exist" to see that long before the publication of *No toda es vigilia,* Macedonio's metaphysics was exercising considerable influence.

In the December 1924 issue we find one of Borges's most fervent endorsements of Macedonio's talent. It appears in an essay called "Después de las imágenes" ("After Images"). The last paragraph reads:

The image is sorcery. To transform a bonfire into a tempest, as Milton does, is the work of a wizard. To change the moon into a fish, into a bubble, into a kite—as Rossetti did, falling into error even before Lugones—is a lesser prank. There is someone who is superior to the wizard and the prankster. I am talking about the demigod, the angel, whose work transforms the world. To add provinces to Being, to hallucinate cities and spaces of conjoined reality, is an heroic adventure. Buenos Aires has not as yet achieved its poetic immortalization. On the pampa, a gaucho once stood up to the devil in a competition of song; in Buenos Aires nothing has happened so far, and its greatness has not as yet been certified by a symbol, an astonishing fable, or even an individual story comparable to that of Martin Fierro. I do not know whether or not there is a divine will at work in the world, but if it exists, the pink warehouse, this succulent spring, and the red gas meter were conceived by it. . . . I should like to note two approximations to the fabulization of the city: One is the poem woven by the tangos—a precarious and vulgar whole, which distorts the life of the people into parodies and which recognizes no characters but the tough guys of the nostalgic past and no activity but prostitution; the other is the brilliant, oblique humor of Macedonio Fernández's Recienvenido.

Borges's veneration of Macedonio during this period is well known, for he has made no secret of it: "In those days I imitated him to the point of transcription, to the extreme of impassioned and devout plagiarism," he said at Macedonio's tomb. The poet Pedro Juan Vignale once jokingly referred to Borges as "el Platón inconfeso de Macedonio Fernández," so notorious did this idolatry become. Ulyses Petit de Murat, recalling this remark, concurs: "Borges is so much the unconfessed Plato of Macedonio Fernández these days that he hardly writes anything without mentioning him; he repeats his witticisms wherever he goes; he takes us to visit him, to shake him out of the Idealist contemplation into which he sinks, his windows perpetually closed, a guitar at hand for playing

Bach and papers written on in every direction scattered about his little room, which is in a nondescript boarding-house in Buenos Aires" ("La revolución literaria de *Martín Fierro*," p. 13). The identities of this Plato and his Socrates may have been as mysteriously intertwined at that moment as those of their Athenian forebears, but we ought to say at once that the adjective "unconfessed" could only have been used in jest. Borges has repeatedly revealed his debt to Macedonio Fernández in statements expressing both admiration for a man of genius and tenderness toward a gentle *padre espiritual*.

Macedonio, for his part, admired Borges's talent, calling him on one occasion "the most gifted prose writer in the Spanish language in my incompetent judgment." He goes on to say:

> As for Banchs, and especially for Borges, all one knows of them is their intelligence, as is the case with Jiménez; the desire to hide his individual vicissitude (not the same as wanting to look good) is a piquant idiosyncracy of Borges, who has a secretive temperament, excessively given to ferreting out individual strayings and vicissitudes, which are, after all, what destinies are made of, destinies being art's greatest love. (*Proa*, second cycle 1:16)

Borges eventually came to regret the influence that Macedonio had upon his style, and his estimation of Macedonio's work has undergone an evolution in the course of the last twenty years that parallels his rejection of much of his own early work: inevitably, Macedonio is associated in his mind with "the Ultraist error." His most recent assessment of Macedonio's influence appeared in his "Autobiographical Notes" in the September 1970 *New Yorker*:

His chief gift to me was to make me read skeptically. At the outset, I plagiarized him devotedly, picking up certain stylistic mannerisms of his that I later came to regret. I look back on him now, however, as an Adam bewildered by the Garden of Eden. His genius survives in but a few of his pages; his influence was of a Socratic nature. I truly loved the man, on this side idolatry, as much as any.

There would be much to explore in a study of the affinities of the two writers and their influence upon each other. Whether they spoke of Schopenhauer or Heraclitus, their discussions led them perpetually to the brink of the same abyss: the mystery of human identity. What each beheld therein we can never know precisely, but, inexplicably, certain visions of a selfless universe that one of them found atrocious became for the other a source of illumination. The importance of these discussions for the work of both men cannot be overestimated.

Martín Fierro; la Revista Oral; the Presidential Campaign.

"Everything is new under the sun," said Oliverio Girondo in the manifesto he wrote for *Martín Fierro,* "if you look at it with today's eyes and express it in a contemporary accent." Nothing could be more in keeping with the *martinfierrista* spirit than the vision of Recienvenido, "Adam bewildered by the Garden of Eden," who somehow perceived the world as it had never been perceived before: a world where a man could buy a new cane already lost and save himself the trouble of losing it, where the front halves of automobiles had been eliminated by manufacturers in order to prevent collisions, and where thick books were sold already read and very good books already returned by the friends most likely to borrow them. The world seen by Macedonio delighted the *martinfierristas,* and although his humor, unlike theirs, was never a weapon for ridicule or humiliation, he could be as irreverent as the best of them. Who among them would have suggested at this time, the moment of the apotheosis of Martín Fierro, the glorious hour of Don Segundo Sombra, that he suspected that the gaucho had been created primarily as an entertainment for horses?

Macedonio's work was in great demand, but he was a reluctant collaborator. Evar Méndez, editor of *Martín Fierro,* writing in *Contrapunto* in 1945, recalls:

> By then Macedonio Fernández was an authoritative and respected colleague . . . and from this precursor of the movement for the renovation of ideas, of poetry, of language, in which we were all engaged, I took some early poems I had discovered in which he seemed to anticipate all this, and reprinted them. From time to time the fervor and admiration of the younger generation prevailed and pages of his humorous writing were snatched away from him and published, his reputation gradually increasing. . . . Finally these were gathered together, providing the bulk of the material in *Papeles de Recienvenido* [*Newcomer's Papers*], published by my Cuadernos del Plata in 1929. (*Contrapunto* 1:8–14)

Méndez's denomination of Macedonio as "precursor" has never been seriously disputed and is accepted by most critics. Mario Trejo's comments on "Suave encantamiento" are typical:

> It is said that in 1913 when Apollinaire published

"Alcools," twentieth-century poetry was officially inaugurated with the (now famous) image, "The window opens like an orange/ the beautiful fruit of light." And nevertheless, in 1904 Macedonio Fernández had already written in "Soft Enchantment": "Eyes that open like mornings, and, closing, let evening fall," an image which brought words together, (not merely words, but their emotive charge as well) in a much more provocative way than Apollinaire had done.[9]

Paradoxically, the "precursor of Ultraism" published only one other poem before 1942: the sketchy version of "Elena Bellamuerte" included by Borges, Huidobro, and Hidalgo in *Indice de la nueva poesía americana* in 1926. Macedonio's poems probably circulated in manuscript, however, and may have been known to his circle of friends long before they appeared in print. Moreover, a few short prose pieces were published in *Martín Fierro,* and little by little Macedonio was persuaded to publish in other periodicals, including some of the zaniest literary ventures of the avant-garde.

The era, so prodigal in the creation of magazines, begat not only a famous mural magazine (which "no one read, not even the walls," according to Borges), but also the ultimate in periodicals, Alberto Hidalgo's *Revista Oral,* which noisily "went to press" in the basement of the café Royal Keller as each of the contributors read aloud the passionate or hilarious paragraphs prepared for the occasion. "Trials" of Lugones and Gerchunoff (whose defense attorney was Borges) and Macedonio's incomparable "Carta abierta uruguaya-argentina" ("Open Uruguayan-Argentine Letter") were memorable features. Lafleur, Provenzano, and Alonso list the founders as follows: "The *Revista Oral* was founded by Alberto Hidalgo, along with Macedonio Fernández, Norah Lange, Carlos Pérez Ruiz, Francisco Luis Bernárdez, Emilio Pettoruti, Roberto A. Ortelli, Raúl Scalabrini Ortiz, Brandán Caraffa, Eduardo González Lanuza, Leopoldo Marechal, and Jorge Luis Borges" (pp. 104–5).

In 1927 Macedonio waged a campaign for the presidency of Argentina. Is it conceivable that shy, obscure Macedonio could possibly have been in earnest in contending for his country's highest office? Or was it all a hoax, an ingenious exercise in avant-garde humor, the ultimate absurdity being electoral victory for a nonexistent candidate? It is tempting to dismiss the whole affair as *martinfierrista* high jinks, but his friends insist that, all things considered, Macedonio seemed to take the whole matter very seriously for a joke, if joke it were. Whether hoax or giant metaphor, the campaign waged by Macedonio Fernández in 1927 is certainly the strangest in the history of democratic institutions.

Macedonio spurned customary forms of propaganda in favor of the personal approach. To make his name known, he hit upon the clever scheme of "forgetting" wherever he went small strips of paper on which he had written in longhand the single word "Macedonio." He soon enlarged upon this idea, as explained in a letter to Fernández Latour:

We must advertise. I prefer to do it by giving the appearance of having an affair of the heart. This way it will have a certain intrigue and it won't seem like propaganda. This sort of thing:

Macedonio is looking for Casilda, the Cuban. Please call Rivadavia 3729.

Every morning I put in my pocket a dozen squares of
paper with this message written on them in blue or
red pencil. (Latour, "Macedonio Fernández")

His rationale was indisputable: "I believe that my appeal
is more powerful than the kind you find in big newspapers,
for since it is intriguing, people talk about it with their
friends; besides, since it doesn't seem like propaganda, the
paper goes on circulating."

The plans of the candidate and his "staff" included the
composition of a fantastic novel, set in Buenos Aires,
entitled "El hombre que será presidente" (" The Man who
Will Be President"), of which Borges gives an entertaining
account in the prologue to his anthology *Macedonio
Fernández*. The strategy envisioned by the collaborators
(Borges, the Dabove brothers, Carlos Pérez Ruiz, Fernández Latour, and Macedonio) was Machiavellian indeed.
In the novel, as well as in the "real" campaign, the first
step was to undermine the spiritual equilibrium of every
citizen through the introduction of a series of sinister
inventions, such as the steep stairway of unequal stairs, the
tissue-paper soup spoon, the detachable lapel (which came
off in the hand of an eager interlocutor) and the automatic
sugar dispenser which sullenly refused to release sugar.
Most sinister of all was the movable spittoon, which
perversely sidled left or right, ensuring the humiliation of
the most accomplished spitter. When the wretched
populace had been brought to its knees by these insane
artifacts, the all powerful righter-of-wrongs, Macedonio
Fernández, was to appear upon the scene, promising
swift return to a life of peace and prosperity.

A last stage of the campaign outlined by Macedonio in
a letter to Fernández Latour, must certainly have been

Argentina's introduction to the "happening," had it been carried out:

> In politico-literary affairs, I have but one thought for this year: that of carrying out your beautiful idea of a theatrical event, the theory of the living novel, the presentation of live characters. . . . My plan, based on your suggestion, is to act out a novel in the streets of Buenos Aires, in homes, restaurants, etc.—a novel (or at least important scenes of one, making the public believe that it is really taking place). . . . (Latour, "Macedonio Fernández").

Here lies a possible explanation of Macedonio's unaccountable earnestness. The campaign was "un asunto literario-político." And the "literary" aspects of a presidential campaign—an area where life and fiction melt one into the other—interested him deeply. The conscious fabrication of an identity, the whole process of mythologization that characterizes the "making" of a president, were endlessly fascinating to him *as literary projects*. The political aspects of the campaign, it is hardly necessary to mention, were of considerably less importance. "The mechanism of fame interested him, not its attainment," Borges concludes in his prologue.

And yet the idea of *being* president never lost its fascination. Decades after Yrigoyen "defeated" Macedonio, a certain *Presidente* came into the spotlight as central character in the novel *Museo de la novela de la Eterna*. It is not difficult to identify him as one of the shy author's numerous *personae*.

Not a literary movement in the usual sense, *martinfierrismo* was primarily unified, according to Leopoldo Marechal, by its undeniable élan. In reality there was no unanimous aesthetic creed. "What held us together was an attitude toward life, a joy, a euphoria, a desire to change things, to accomplish things. Therefore, once the combative phase of the movement had ended, each of us went his own way" (García, *Hablan de Macedonio Fernández,* p. 72). The high-spirited camaraderie, the ebullience, the combativeness that characterized *martinfierrismo* were powerful stimulants. Macedonio, as *contertulio* of the *martinfierristas,* not only lent considerable candlepower to their brilliance, but was in turn affected by his contact with them. There can be little doubt that some of his finest pages were written—and have been preserved—because of his association with these lively kindred spirits.

Publication; Macedonio and His Papers.

An often repeated article of faith in the Macedonian mythology is the belief that neither the elaboration of his work nor its publication interested him in the slightest. This notion is repeated, for example, in Borges's romantic portrait of Macedonio:

Writing was not a chore for Macedonio Fernández. To a greater extent than any person I have ever known he lived to think. He abandoned himself each day to the surprises and vicissitudes of thought, as a swimmer to a great river, and that mode of thinking which is called writing did not cost him the slightest effort. (Prologue to *Macedonio Fernández*)

Borges goes on to recount Macedonio's custom of leaving great stacks of papers behind whenever he moved to a new furnished room—something he did every few months—and concludes: "Macedonio did not ascribe the slightest value to his writings."

This statement does not seem to hold true for all of Macedonio's writing, but it does seem to apply to his note-taking or journal-keeping activity. Macedonio did indeed "live to think," and, as we have noted, wrote constantly, filling notebook upon notebook (started at both ends and in several "middles") with the fruits of his meditations. In Macedonio's words, quoted previously, "I write for myself, not because I need to speak, to use words, in order to think, but in order to stimulate my mind and to preserve signs for evocation." This dialogue with himself was constant, and it was perhaps inevitable that in the course of time the same themes should occur again and again. Chided by Borges for not taking pains to preserve and organize his papers, Macedonio told him that to believe that an idea can be lost "is an idle boast, since the human mind is so poor that it is condemned always to find, to lose and to rediscover the same things, over and over." Friends who were not so certain of this made desperate attempts to salvage manuscripts, but Adolfo de Obieta estimates that more of his father's papers have been lost than saved.

But a distinction must be made between the running dialogues Macedonio carried on with himself as an aid to meditation, and the manuscripts intended for publication. If the first type of writing "did not cost him the slightest effort," the second cost him dearly. He called his writing-table "a martyr's block" and once described a book as "the most fragile, intractable, irritating, tedious-to-make torture device, destined to perpetually frustrate and disappoint. . . ."

A study of the genesis of certain works, *Museo de la novela de la Eterna*, for example, reveals a long and arduous

process of elaboration and revision. By comparing successive versions of poems, Nélida Salvador has demonstrated
that Macedonio was much more the patient and con-
scientious craftsman than he is ordinarily given credit for
being.

Macedonio, then, was *not* equally indifferent to the fate
of all his papers. Adolfo de Obieta has indicated that there
are numerous manuscripts on which Macedonio even left
instructions to his future editor: "Adolfo, if you get
around to publishing this some day," something he would
hardly have done if it were strictly true that he ascribed no
value to his writings.

Macedonio's work habits were rather unusual. Extremely sensitive to cold, he worked best when swathed in
layer upon layer of sweaters, ponchos, and scarves. On his
head he might wear a knitted cap, a bowler, a fur hat, or
a towel, and a continuous supply of scalding *mate* was
necessary to fend off the chill. He wrote on whatever paper
was at hand, occasionally in two directions, both horizon-
tally and vertically. He kept certain pages in a container
which he called in "incubator" where they might "age".
The incubated papers were later reworked, certain themes
being elaborated in dozens of different versions. Already
published pieces were also revised in several versions with
copious marginal notes. He seemed to prefer to keep all
his work in a constant state of flux. The editor's dream of
a definitive edition would have been abhorrent to him,
completely foreign to the spirit and praxis of his art.

It is regrettable that Macedonio Fernández did not
possess to a greater degree the ability to come to practical
terms with his theories and to organize his ideas effectively.
There is no doubt that the lack of this ability was a serious
impediment to the realization of his art. A procrastinating
perfectionist whose literary ideal would be a kind of

perpetually fluid improvisation, he was a victim both of his temperament and of his own nearly impossible-to-realize theories. Macedonio abominated above all else "the empty and perfect book." His literary history appears to be an infinite series of ploys to avoid its creation.

Principal Works (1928-53).

Each of the six books prepared for publication before Macedonio's death in 1952 points in some way toward *La novela de la Eterna*. The first, *No toda es vigilia la de los ojos abiertos,* reveals the cosmos in which Macedonio would create his fictional worlds, including that of Eterna. Published in 1928 by Gleizer, *No toda es vigilia* has the distinction of being the only one of his books that Macedonio published voluntarily. Subtitled *A Collection of Papers Left by a Character in a Novel, Deunamor, the Non-existent Gentleman, Expert in Expectation,* the book is a rhapsodic metaphysical essay with occasional fictional interludes. It is a much more serious book than its subtitle would suggest, for in it Macedonio reveals the essential tenets of his metaphysics. No attempt is made to present these ideas in a logically structured form; in fact, something of the opposite is true: *No toda es vigilia* is, among other things, a satirical attack upon traditional philosophical exposition. By turns waggish, lyrical, and profound, Macedonio wrestles with the venerable problems of Idealism and resolves them by means of some perplexing assertions regarding the self. The title refers to the book's central thesis, "Ojos abiertos no son todo vigilia ni toda la vigilia," which is sustained in a variety of ways, including the use of fictional episodes, such as the lively debate between the philosopher Hobbes and a certain "neighborhood metaphysician," Macedonio Fernández. *No toda es vigilia* is central to our study of Macedonio's theory of art, and a consideration of its principal ideas will be the subject of the next chapter.

Papeles de Recienvenido appeared in 1929. Prepared by Borges and "pulcramente editado" by Alfonso Reyes for Evar Méndez's Cuadernos del Plata, the book was a collection of humorous articles Macedonio had published between 1922 and 1929 in *La Gaceta del Sur, Martín Fierro, Proa,* and *Pulso.* The unifying element in this book —never conceived as a book by its author—is its style. Luis Alberto Sánchez notes:

> In *Papeles de Recienvenido* . . . we can see what Ramón [Gómez de la Serna] was alluding to: a metaphysics of nonsense (I would say of "metanonsense"), which Macedonio considered the characteristic expression of the native of this hemisphere. If it can be compared with anything at all it is with the digressive technique of Cantinflas. . . . To speak for the sake of lulling time to sleep and deflecting ideas is something which is very much a part of us and of any creature on the defensive, whose heroism consists of being most intractable when he is in the greatest danger.[10]

Macedonio's exploitation of the possibilities inherent in the ancient comic device of digression is one of the major discoveries of his art, a discovery that had important implications for his stories and novels. To progress logically, to move a narrative forward chronologically, is merely to bring the reader closer to its, and his, end. According to Macedonio, to perpetually digress, to manage to avoid arriving at the inevitable "next morning" in a narrative, is to beguile time itself, to add a new dimension to the reader's existence.

From the digressions of Recienvenido to the narrative style of *Una novela que comienza* (*A Novel which Begins*) is but a step, a possibility that Borges seems to have divined. In his premature review of "El Recienvenido," Borges had written in 1923: "In the digressions of Macedonio Fernández I seem to see an imagination in constant exercise: an activity which buoyantly goes on designing universes, not regimented and fatal like a chess problem, but impromptu and mischievous like a good game of truco." In *Una novela que comienza* Macedonio applies Recienvenido's ingenious ploys to the creation of some unusual fiction.

Credit for salvaging the manuscripts of *Una novela que comienza* belongs to the Peruvian Alberto Hidalgo. Hidalgo's compatriot Luis Alberto Sánchez promoted the project of publishing the work in Chile. In 1941 Sánchez edited the work for Ercilla and provided an amusing and perceptive prologue. Sánchez assembled a curious miscellany of tales, prologues, and fragmentary pieces. The result is a kind of writer's notebook, invaluable in tracing the course of Macedonio's interest in fiction. He tells us that his narratives are experiments in radical "aesthetic research," attempts to discover an "extremely severe Art," which would be "exempt from conventionality and from appeal to the senses."

Two of the narrations in this volume, the title story and "Tantalia," can certainly be said to meet Macedonio's own stringent requirements. "Tantalia" is the story of a young man whose lover gives him a clover plant to tend in order to "reeducate his sensibility." Unaccountably, the youth finds himself driven to commit acts of torture upon this most vulnerable of nature's creations; in a paroxysm of cruelty, he deprives the tiny plant of moisture. His unconscionable behavior threatens the existence of the cosmos: "Without its even being carried out, the very thought of such a deed in a human mind is sufficient to cause all that exists to tremble on the brink of Nonbeing." For its lyric quality, "Tantalia" was included in the 1953 edition of Macedonio's poetry. For the originality of its conceptions, the story was included in the famous *Antología de la literatura fantástica* prepared by Jorge Luis Borges, Silvina Ocampo, and Adolfo Bioy Casares. It is a story that can indeed be said to be *"exento de convencionalidad."*

In "Una novela que comienza," dated 1921, Macedonio's digressions turn lyrical as he begins a love story, or would-be love story, all the more evocative because it never progresses beyond the initial melancholy yearnings of the characters. The composition is all prelude, consisting of nothing more substantial than the reverie of a middle-aged man vaguely attracted by a young woman whom he has never met. Nothing whatever happens to these ethereal characters; the author resolutely prevents the elements of the narrative from crystallizing into a conventional story. In this sense "Una novela que comienza" is a clear precedent for the radical experimentation undertaken in *Museo de la novela de la Eterna.*

In 1942 some of Macedonio's poetry was collected by Marcos Fingerit in a tiny volume "of Franciscan presence" entitled *Muerte es Beldad (Death is Beauty)*. Among the admirers of *Muerte es Beldad* was Juan Ramón Jiménez, who wrote in *La corriente infinita:*

> Many years ago I discovered and read Macedonio Fernández. Wherever I have found anything of his, I have devoured it. . . . The elements which Macedonio Fernández discovers in life and death and out of which he creates his phenomenon are always first-rate, both in idea and in feeling. And his language is an

Esperanto of a definitive place where each one of us speaks his own language and where we all, without philologists, understand one another. Incomparable. He stands with Dante, Blake, Eliot. (p. 186)

The Losada edition of *Papeles de Recienvenido; Continuación de la nada* (*Newcomer's Papers; Continuation of Nothing*)* appeared in 1944. It was Macedonio's fifth book and the last to be published during his lifetime. This edition included a prologue by Ramón Gómez de la Serna—an enlargement of his 1937 article in *Sur* that he hoped would be Macedonio's "passport to fame." The previous edition of *Papeles de Recienvenido* had been limited to 465 copies, "all given away," according to Macedonio. The Losada edition is greatly enlarged (279 pages as compared to 74 pages in the 1929 edition) and contains a long essay on humor (which will interest us in a later chapter as we examine Macedonio's theory of art). "Para una teoría de la humorística" ("Toward a Theory of Humor") is a provocative and original analysis of the dynamics of humor. Macedonio's study of humor has the extraordinary advantage of having been written by a humorist, an attribute not shared by the well-known studies by Freud, Bergson, Lipps, and company (whose work Macedonio had studied with scholarly thoroughness).

The section entitled "Temas del libro que se despide" ("Themes of a Departing Book") contains one of Macedonio's best-known and most perfect tales, "El zapallo que se hizo cosmos" ("The Squash That Became the Cosmos"). This is the story of a squash that, finding its optimum conditions for growth, grew and grew, absorbing into itself not only rivers, deserts, and mountains, but

*Hereafter cited as PR44.

all the races of mankind. All things in the world were
eventually included within the huge hollow of its yellow
shell; therein we—all of us—dwell even now. According
to the doctrine of "cucurbitaceous (squashly) metaphysics," our completely self-contained system, having, as
it does, exclusively internal relations," is a deathless
world:

> The Squash has permitted me to write for you,
> dear brothers of the Order of Squashliness, albeit
> poorly and inadequately, its history and its legend.
> We live in the world which we have always known,
> but we are now all within the shell, with purely
> internal relations, and hence, without death. (PR66,
> p. 163)

It is probable that this edition of *Papeles de Recienvenido*,
published when the author was seventy years old, was the
general public's first introduction to Macedonio Fernández.
Two other stories, published in magazines, will be of
interest to us as we consider Macedonio's narrative theory.
"Cirugía psíquica de extirpación" ("Surgery of Psychic
Removal"), the story of a man whose sense of futurity is
removed surgically, provides in a series of running foot-
notes nearly as long as the story a puckish commentary on
the art of storytelling. Commenting all the while on his
own craft, the author proceeds to tell us the story of hapless
Cósimo Schmitz, incapable, after his operation, of
conceiving of more than eight minutes of future time.
This doubling back of the narrative upon itself is a technique that Macedonio will exploit fully in *Museo de la
novela de la Eterna*.
The second story, "Donde Solano Reyes era un vencido
y sufría dos derrotas cada día" ("In Which Solano Reyes

Was a Defeated Man and Suffered Two Losses Every Day"), is an account of the way in which the "eternities" of a moribund old man and his young niece are mysteriously linked to an infinite chain of loaves of freshly baked bread, corroborating the story's Macedonian thesis: "Death is not fatal." Here again the author appears as author in the story, pointing out to the reader certain excellences of the narration.

In 1943 Macedonio and his two sons, Jorge and Adolfo, embarked upon an enterprise that was to be both enjoyable for them and significant in the history of Argentine literature. In *Las revistas literarias argentinas* we read:

> One evening in the spring of 1943 casual visitors to those all-night bookstores on Corrientes had what was certainly a most pleasurable surprise: there in their hands was a newborn magazine. This was not a poetry magazine in which a group of young people launched a manifesto. Neither did it postulate any militant position against the social and political realities of the day. As he made his way through its pages, the reader, now over his initial surprise, discovered that he had at last encountered what had been lacking in the intellectual climate of Buenos Aires. It was as if from some hidden place in the city this lively spirit had suddenly burst forth into the street, full of irony and humor, but at the same time serious and profound. Even at a distance one could detect a certain family resemblance, a peculiar style of putting words together which formed the hinges of a clever prose of humorous bent; one could see that its lineage could be traced to only one possible source: Macedonio Fernández. (p. 195)

The magazine was *Papeles de Buenos Aires*. The indefinable, unmistakable stamp of Macedonio was to be found on every one of its large, handsome pages. Readers, for example, are invited to submit manuscripts in the following terms:

(Whether or not you are brilliant, send us your manuscript or your opinion about something. Above all, criticize. There is nothing sadder than not existing.) All we ask of contributors is that they maintain a minimum amount of self-doubt.

To think, to risk having an original idea in the midst of this obsessive world, to experience the freedom to be, to think daringly and fervently; to study and dream of reality with patience and affection.

Compiled and edited with a serendipitous abundance of intelligence, humor, and imagination, *Papeles de Buenos Aires* was more than a family closet full of pleasant surprises. Collaborators included Enrique Molina, Jules Supervielle, Ulyses Petit de Murat, Eduardo Keller, Olga Orozco, and many others. *Papeles de Buenos Aires* has among many distinctions that of having introduced to its readers the fiction of Witold Gombrowicz. Many of Macedonio's contributions are unsigned, but it is not difficult to recognize him as "Pensador Poco," "Pensador Corto," and the owner of several other peculiar pseudonyms. Originals by Adolfo and Jorge de Obieta— philosophy, poetry and humor—maintained *Papeles's* distinctive literary blend from issue to issue:

Jorge and Adolfo de Obieta, the sons of Macedonio Fernández, shared richly the family manner of spying upon the world from such an original, Quevedesque angle, and the pages they edited for each issue brought the unexpected and the subtle, providing a welcome oasis in which to rest from the literature of the literati. (*Las revistas literarias argentinas*, p. 196)

The last volume in the cycle of works prepared for publication during Macedonio's lifetime was *Poemas*, published posthumously in 1953. A nearly complete collection of his poetry, *Poemas* was published in Mexico by Guarania. Natalicio González prepared the prologue and Cofeen Serpa the illustrations. This volume includes many poems not included in *Muerte es Beldad* and closes with the lyrical tale "Tantalia." This book established beyond question Macedonio's right to a permanent niche in the Argentina pantheon of poets.

Eterna's Novelist

In 1947 Macedonio ended his dreary quarter-century tour of the boardinghouses of Buenos Aires and went to live with his son Adolfo in a pleasant apartment facing the Botanical Gardens. "Once again my father had a home," Adolfo writes,

> . . . and at last had something more than what had constituted his wordly possessions for a quarter of a century: a bed, a table, a chair, a guitar; now he had an easy chair, a piano, and a library and two windows looking out upon a beautiful street, and, why hide it, for he would like me to be faithful, a little corner where he dreamed a lot, where he kept himself warm, and thought and even wrote: now he had a little kitchen. ("Mi padre, Macedonio Fernández," p. 147)

In the warm kitchen corner provided by Adolfo, Macedonio, now seventy-three, continued writing and rewriting with no sense of urgency successive versions of *La novela de la Eterna*. Adolfo encouraged his father with all the persuasive power at his disposal to complete the project, but the pages accumulated with little apparent order as the days of Macedonio's life slipped away. In one of the prologues, however, he wryly noted:

> The greatest risk one runs in publishing a novel at this stage in life is that someone may not know your age: mine is 73, and I hope that in stating this I may stave off a prospective critical opinion, such as: ". . . this being the author's first novel, we predict for him a promising future if he perseveres in his artistic endeavors with a firm will and sound discipline. At any rate, we shall await his future works before making a definitive judgment." With this kind of delay I shall be left without posterity. (*Museo de la novela de la Eterna* [hereafter cited as M], p. 19)

Reflecting upon his father's strengths and weaknesses, Adolfo de Obieta observes:

> Providence endowed him richly with a sense of mystery, poetry, humor, analytical powers, conceptual rigor, imagination, with a strange polyvalence for metaphysics, science, poetry, and art; but much less richly did it endow him in character, discipline, and, perhaps, appropriate environment. His work could have been considerably more important, because he had a mind to which much that is human and something that is divine were not foreign. A certain lack of discipline, a certain nonconcern for

time, perhaps a certain conviction that, sooner or later the microcosm will be identical with the macrocosm anyway, or a certain disdain for the glories of the world, or a certain lack of necessary vanity, which I in my juvenile way used to reproach him for, reminding him that inaction can be worse than an actual wrong action; some or all of these factors may explain why many written pages and several unwritten books in many degrees of semiexistence have simply been lost. ("Mi padre, Macedonio Fernández," p. 150)

La novela de la Eterna continued to exist inchoate, or in darying degrees of inchoateness, "the papers not semiorganized, but quarti- or octavi-organized," in Obieta's words. Inevitably, Macedonio penned one day the final word. He died following a brief illness on February 10, 1952.

It has been observed that as an object of knowledge, a literary work has "a special ontological status, being neither real (physical, like a statue), nor mental (psychological, like the experience of light or pain), nor ideal (like a triangle). . . ."[11] What, then, can we say of the mode of existence of Macedonio's eternally incipient novel? Dreamed by the author, recorded by him in infinite versions, fashioned by Adolfo de Obieta into one of many possible forms, the work still depends very much for its completion upon the active participation of the reader. Given its aesthetic, it seems appropriate that the work should manifest itself in precisely this indefinable fashion.

One wonders whether there may not have been as much wiliness as *abulia* behind Macedonio's disinclination to "finish" *La novela de la Eterna*. The apparently bemused old man dreaming beside the stove, casually brushing pages to the floor as if they were ashes from his cigar, must certainly have relished this delicious pose. Notorious throughout his life for his *picardías*, for the fine irony of his words and deeds, he was after all the same old man who scrawled in the margins of many of these pages, "Adolfo, if you get around to publishing this some day..." or "In case I die. . . ."

It is conceivable that Macedonio wished to leave the novel in precisely this indeterminate state. He had taken evident delight in the novel's long "mythological" existence. He remarks in the prologue called "Andando":

> A novel whose very existence is novelesque because it has been announced, promised, and withdrawn so many times; and the reader who can understand it will be novelesque as well. Such a reader will become famous and will be classified as the fantastic reader. He will be very widely read, by all the various publics of readers, this reader of mine. (M, p. 21)

More importantly, the potentiality for permutation was an essential aspect of the novel, or "text-in-the-making," as Macedonio conceived it. The last chapter of the novel, called "Final Prologue," is addressed "TO WHOEVER WOULD LIKE TO WRITE THIS NOVEL." In it Macedonio invites each reader to try his hand at making a novel out of the elements provided, elements that are, he says, "rich in suggestions" (M, p. 236).

In *No toda es vigilia* Macedonio had written: "We could as well say that the one who is writing (or feels that he is writing) here is you and the one who is reading, I" (*No toda* [hereafter cited as NTV], p. 175). In the usual configuration author/book/reader, such a statement could only be a literary conceit, and not a particularly original one. But Macedonio Fernández is not writing in accordance with this convention—quite the reverse. For him the identification "Yo/tú" is not figurative but real, having its basis in the indivisibility of consciousness: "Every state of consciousness falls within a single identifying chain; you do not possess, nor do you know any personal series save one, which you call yours, and this belongs to the only field of consciousness that exists" (NTV, p. 173). Much of *Museo* is a dramatization of the belief that there is a universal consciousness, that it is one, and that all that occurs is sensed by it alone. A difficult concept for the Western reader, conditioned from birth to think of the self as "encapsuled by the skin," and of the books he reads as similarly enclosed, tidily bound within *some* kind of hide.

The book that would illumine Macedonio's view of consciousness could not itself be permanently bound. All things considered, the open structure of *Museo* is uniquely suited for the expression of its essential ideas. Our concepts of "author," "reader," and "personage" are linked to a number of unspoken convictions concerning the self and the nature of individual consciousness—convictions so much a part of the way we experience the world that we assume that they are self-evident, universal principles. Macedonio, however, leads us into a disturbing world in which "reader," "author," "personage"— "you," "I," and our aesthetic projections—are no longer discrete entities, no longer operate according to a familiar dynamic. The strangeness we encounter in the novelistic world of Macedonio Fernández is not a mere strangeness of diction; rather, it manifests a much more fundamental strangeness of conception.

Any attempt to penetrate the world of la Eterna must

begin with an examination of Macedonio's fundamental
metaphysical assumptions, especially his ideas concerning
the nature of the self. We shall look next at some of
these ideas, considering what implications they may
have for a theory of the novel.

A very long period of gestation produced the author of
the novel of la Eterna. Antinovelist or archnovelist,
Macedonio fancied himself the curator of a vast "Museo
de la Novela," not a display of petrified remains, but an
open diorama of the novel-in-the-making: a fitting
reliquary for his disconcerting discoveries.

Chapter II

A Combative Idealism

Macedonio's metaphysical writings are seditious; they are the thoughts of a man deeply distressed by the world view common to his time and place in history and eager to effect a change. His dissatisfaction is much more radical than the nearly universal reaction of men of his generation against the sterility of the prevailing positivist theory. Macedonio's metaphysics, nourished, we should like to suggest, by what certainly appear to be mystical experiences, contests the most fundamental assumptions of Western thought. What is undertaken in *No toda es vigilia* is nothing less than "the liberation of human thought from . . . impure shadows" (NTV, pp. 85–86). These "impure shadows"—notions of a real world, real time, and a real self transcendent to experience—are precisely the shadows his combative aesthetics will attempt to exorcise; in examining the narrative art of Macedonio Fernández, a consideration of his metaphysical suppositions is therefore essential. His belief in the parity of image and sensation, his belief in the illusory nature of the self, his Vendatic view of consciousness, birth, and death, are not easily inferred from his novel alone, and each of these notions has a direct bearing on some significant aspect of his craft. The shortest route to *Museo de la novela de la Eterna* may thus be the circuitous path through *No toda es vigilia la de los ojos abiertos.*

In examining Macedonio's metaphysics, we are fortunate to have a variety of texts to consider. By far the most important of these is the long essay, *No toda es vigilia la de los ojos abiertos,* published in 1928. In a greatly enlarged edition of this work published in 1967,* Adolfo de Obieta has included many other articles and previously unpublished manuscripts dealing with metaphysical themes. These span a long period of years, from 1908 to 1950, and are helpful in tracing the evolution of Macedonio's thought.

Metaphysics: The Return to "Pure Vision"

Metaphysics, then, proposes to discover the path and the procedure for returning to the Vision, and it assures us that however we regain a state of pure Vision, once we attain it, our curious perplexity will be instantly dissipated and our Intelligence will be fully reconciled to the fact of its existence and of all existence. ("La Metafísica" [1908], NTV, p. 44)

*The Centro Editor edition of *No toda es vigilia* contains, in addition to this work, several other articles on metaphysics, some of them previously unpublished. In citing from these essays we shall give the title and the approximate date of composition. NTV without additional notation will be understood to mean the essay *No toda es vigilia* itself.

In November 1928, shortly after the publication of *No toda es vigilia la de los ojos abiertos,* the philosopher Miguel A. Virasoro wrote to Macedonio:

> With regard to your book, I believe the feeling is unanimous; we are all indebted to the friends who forced you to publish it; it is, in my judgment, the only book of intensely "lived" philosophy which has ever been written in this country. All the others have a pale and bookish life; in yours there is a sense of deep inner drama.

Virasoro's observation is accurate; whatever we may conclude about *No toda es vigilia* as a metaphysical treatise, the vitality of the work is undeniable: *No toda es vigilia* has a quality of firsthand personal testimony. *Metafísica,* in the special sense in which Macedonio uses the word, is more than a dispassionate, intellectual inquiry into the nature of ultimate reality; it is a passionate, total effort to regain a primordial "pure vision": what is sought is not an explanation of ultimate reality, but an experience of it.

"Pure vision" is ours, according to Macedonio, in the state of prereflective innocence, but as we mature, and selfawareness develops and intensifies, being becomes problematical:

> [We lose] that familiarity, the simple and innate acquiescence with our "being," in spite of the fact that we are nothing else but that very thing, "being," and nothing should be more clear and familiar to us than Reality; and in spite of the fact that our reality ought to be for us as intimate, perspicuous, and transparent as if it had just come out of our own hands, we have the notion that existing somehow requires an Explanation. ("La Metafísica," NTV, p. 43)

We wonder at the existence of the world, wonder that we *are*. Schopenhauer understood the *wonder of being* as a source of pain; Macedonio saw the wonder of being (*el asombro de ser*) not only as pain but as a kind of aberration of the spirit: "That malaise which gives rise to the metaphysical question is the "wonder of being," the wonder of existing. It stems from the fact that it has become impossible for us to perceive a phenomenon in all its purity . . ." (*Ibid.*).

By "perceiving a phenomenon in all its purity" Macedonio means perceiving it independent of notions of time, space, and ego-consciousness. In an early essay we catch a glimpse of such a "vision":

At certain moments of mental plenitude, I forget my "self," my body, my ties, my memories, the past, all the acts and impressions which determined my sense of remoteness and the whole long trajectory of evasion and separation. I feel as if I have always been here or that my existence has just begun. But soon even my own existence becomes a matter which has not the slightest consequence for me; "time," "space," are notions which have vanished; everything occurs without reference to place: there is no near nor separate nor lasting nor persisting nor before nor after.

What, then, do I have before me? Phenomenon, Being in its full reality. ("Bases en Metafísica" [1908], NTV, p. 15)

Self-consciousness yields to a state of undifferentiated awareness, bodily sensations disappear, the webs of time and space are suspended; the perceiver is one with the perceived: ontological perplexities vanish. This state of awareness ("in our day extremely rare") achieved in contemplation—or in a transport of passion—is the threshold of metaphysical enlightenment. *Metafísica* is the name Macedonio gives to the activity that, *by any path,* leads to this threshold.

> Metaphysics proposes to discover the path and the procedure for returning to the Vision, and it assures us that however we regain a state of pure Vision, once we attain it, our curious perplexity will be instantly dissipated, and our Intelligence will be fully reconciled to the fact of its existence and of all existence. ("La Metafísica," NTV, p. 44)

Holding in abeyance for a moment the interesting question of Macedonio's mysticism, let us note that *Metafísica,* as Macedonio uses the word, does not lend itself to a rationally argued presentation. "A genuine ratiocination is not to play a part in my exposition" (NTV, p. 148), Macedonio tells us; his writings are to be taken as "a call to the intuition of the reader"; he is not interested in inculcating a doctrine, but in evoking a response, a way of seeing, in the reader, as one might urge a friend to "see" a hidden possibility in a cleverly made optical illusion. Words are only useful to a point; the ultimate "answer" must be the reader's own response. For metaphysics, Macedonio tells us, is not philosophy or science:

> Metaphysics is knowledge of being, not of the laws, relations, or modes of being; it is precisely the consideration of being without reference to relation or situation. It is the attempt to attain a nonapperceptive vision of Reality.

Science and Philosophy are Apperception; Metaphysics is Vision. ("La Metafísica," NTV, p. 36)

One of the chief targets of *No toda es vigilia* is the
traditional, architectonic exposition of European philosophy, with its solemnly laid foundations and its grave and
orderly development of premises. Macedonio's gadfly
attack upon the ponderous giants of metaphysics is
humorous, but he occasionally stings a vulnerable spot.

If these papers are published, I shall be the fortunate
author of the most orderly book ever presented, for
the word order means "like Reality," and the
latter, Being, means free, without law. What the
well-arranged volumes of Kant or Schopenhauer label
chapters one, two, three, and four—and which turn
out to be standard repetitions, retrogressions, recti-
fications, mutual contradictions, rejections—I desig-
nate, with equal rigor, "Another Approach," "The
Same," "Again," "The Same Again," "Once More,"
"Conclusion" (this last one had been a preface, but
the typesetter realized that in it I exhausted my supply
of ideas, and since, very much in character, I had
already given him all the talking-without-thinking
pages we had room for, his experienced hand changed
the title and location of the section), "Response" (a
few questions), "Solution" (I provide the word,
nothing more). (NTV, p. 76)

This passage—the first paragraph of *No toda es vigilia*—
ought to be sufficient warning to the reader that he is
entering a text calculated to challenge precisely those
principles he believes indispensable in metaphysics—
coherence, consistency, and commitment to the logical

development of premises; a text, in short, that will systematically assault these principles, as notions are successively
affirmed, negated, reiterated, ridiculed, and juxtaposed
with their opposites in an ever-moving sea of suppositions.
Exactly as the meaning of the word "order" in the passage
just quoted has slithered, by the end of the first sentence,
to what might normally be considered its opposite, many
other conceptions elude our attempts to grasp them. A
deliberate contradictoriness seems to be one of the essential
principles of the text. It is as if Macedonio, convinced that
no system can contain his subject, which is "free, without
law," had contrived to write so as to ensure that no
system could arise from his text.

But it would be an error to conclude that there is no
method in operation here. The function of the text is to
work upon the reader, to loosen the hold that his philosophical assumptions have upon him. Frustration and
irritation are strategical arms in this process, for Macedonio
plays relentlessly upon the reader's expectations, his
preconceived notions of the nature of metaphysical
discourse, defeating his every attempt at systematization.
Every principle of unity seems deliberately confounded;
Macedonio is by turns analytical and delphic, humorous
and lyrical, mystical and brash. The unorthodox methods
of exposition should not be passed over lightly; the
mental judo that Macedonio, through his digressions,
contradictions, and nonsequiturs, practices upon the
reader *is* a metaphysics; that is to say, it is, in Macedonio's
view, the closest one can come to metaphysics in words.
The value of a metaphysical text is its usefulness as a
springboard, as incitement to intuit that which, by
Macedonio's definition, cannot be said in words.

To abstract from such a text, as we are about to do, is
a perilous and possibly indefensible undertaking, for the

elusive character of the propositions considered within their mobile context is one of the fundamental elements of Macedonio's metaphysical message. What follows, therefore, is a necessarily deficient and distorted account of certain notions that seem to us to emerge from *No toda es vigilia* after many rereadings, ideas that interest us because of the important implications they have for a theory of literature.

"Plenitude of Being . . ."

At the heart of Macedonio's philosophy is a conviction regarding the nature of being: "Being is always full [*pleno*] in all its states, and this plenitude means not being rooted in a self and having no dependence upon so-called externals or so-called substance" (NTV, p. 87). There are no privileged modes of being: we cannot speak of the "real" and the "really real." Systems that make such distinctions are pernicious; they fill the world with "impure shadows." To hold that behind the real world there exists some other, more real realm is to deny to human beings the fullness of being: man is no more than a phantom in such worlds; like the humiliated protagonist of Borges's "The Circular Ruins," he is a mere reflection of some eternally inaccessible something else. *No toda es vigilia* is above all an attempt to exorcise this "something else" in all its guises—as noumenon, matter, substance, Idea, monad, even deity.

Macedonio states his purpose as follows: "The present publication is inspired mainly by desire to present a protest against 'noumenism' " (NTV, p. 85). It soon becomes evident that this is not his only purpose, and that Kant is not his only enemy; but an attack on Kant is a

good point of departure, for it enables him to speak of
several themes that are important to him. For one thing,
Kant held that noumena, being inaccessible to the senses,
were unknowable. The postulation of an unknowable
world, or rather, of the unknowability of the real world,
was, in Macedonio's view, intolerable: "Agnosticism
and noumenism are the worst products of human intelligence," he says. (By agnosticism he means the belief
that reality cannot be known.)

> We believe that . . . a perfect adaptation of the
> Intelligence to the Phenomenon is obtainable; that it is
> contradictory, absurd, to suppose that Intelligence
> might formulate a question which she herself could be
> unable to answer: such unanswerable questions would
> be wonders more miraculous than Being itself. The
> primary attitude of Intelligence in the face of the
> Phenomenon is that of total solutionability. ("Bases
> en Metafísica," [1908], NTV, p. 20)

In the course of No toda es vigilia Macedonio adroitly
refutes the doctrine of noumena, noting the inconsistency
of affirming the existence of essences of which nothing is
known save their unknowability (NTV, p. 114). Legitimate as this refutation may be, Macedonio was not, as
he claims, the first to voice it, as Virasoro points out in a
review of No toda es vigilia ". . . a protest which [the
author] claims has never been formulated until now,
forgetting that reality in itself, noumenal reality, was
denied by Fichte, the immediate successor of Kant, and
definitively refuted by Hegel, who stamped it with the
pithy phrase 'vacuity in itself'" (p. 225). Virasoro notes
that Macedonio has taken a position "out of the mainstream of modern philosophy" ("al trasmano de la filosofía

moderna"); his statement may be taken as a gentle criticism of the author's somewhat eclectic background in philosophy.*

Macedonio's combativeness toward Kantian metaphysics is at bottom a protest against what he calls "Reality pretending to be more than it is"—not reality, but Reality, which, in the ironclad and deterministic universes of certain philosophers, had acquired the power to intimidate, to reduce man to a shadow:

> Such is the state of things which has been created not by reality, certainly, but by Speculative Thinkers who have inclined toward the transcendence of the external and, proceeding in this search for essences, have arrived at the noumenon, calling it the substance of Matter and of Subjectivity, at which Reality and Consciousness have become phantoms, limited to the category of the First Dream. (NTV, p. 91)

"Noumenists," he says elsewhere, "concede us a life and a consciousness of shadows."

Philosophical thinking ought to lead to a kind of reconciliation, "the perfect acquiescence of the intelligence to

---

*Borges's assessment is more colorful, but we must be careful not to take it too literally. "Erudition seemed to him a vain thing, an ostentatious way of not thinking. . . . It was as if Adam, the first man, were thinking over and solving in Paradise the fundamental problems" (Prologue, p. 10). Appealing as such a characterization may be, it amounts to a total, and unjustifiable, denial of Macedonio's scholarship. His knowledge of philosophy was certainly not that of a professional and was indeed acquired in a hapazard fashion, but Macediono was hardly the barefoot sage Borges portrays. He had read extensively in his youth and was familiar with the thought of the major European pholosophers, as is evident from his work.

being." Instead, some philosophies induce a sense of strangeness, *"una extrañeza entre nosotros y el ser."* Theistic systems are no exception, for like the notions of noumena, and matter, and so forth, the idea of God "diminishes being": "The plenitude of being is my doctrine, and this supreme consciousness is not achieved in the subalternation of living with gods" (NTV, p. 103).

Pantheism, in Macedonio's view, is merely a pusillanimous form of materialism *("El panteísmo es la forma más tímida del materialismo")*, and leads inevitably to the same sort of estrangement that materialism does. Macedonio makes no mention of religion as such in any of his writings, yet it would appear that he considered it not the symbolic binding together of all experience, but simply another wedge into the breach, one that produces its own kind of estrangement.

Reality is not a mystery, Macedonio is fond of saying. There is no enigma to be solved; the answer lies at the foot of the question.

> Plainer than Day
>   is Being,
> the fullness of our being,
> everlasting,
> individual and memorious,
> without beginning, without break, without end.
>   (NTV, p. 75)

"Being must be perfectly intelligible" (NTV, p. 35), Macedonio tells us. No doctrine of unknowable worlds, no theological dogma must be permitted to keep us from "seeing" "what is plainer than day."

At the heart of Macedonio's philosophy, then, is his conviction that "being is always full [*pleno*] in all of its states." This conviction, which seems less a philosophical idea than a kind of revelation, must have been a constant source of new insights, for he returns to it again and again, always seeming to discover something more. Most of his important ideas flow from this source. His Idealism, for example, is an elaboration of the notion that "this plenitude means . . . no dependence upon and no correlation with so-called externals and so-called substance." The mystic awareness of which he speaks is the experience which teaches that "this plenitude means not rooted in a self." His insistence on the authority of the dream state is an extension of his belief in "the plenitude of our being in all its states" ("Dreaming and waking are not *degrees* of consciousness . . . ").

His belief in immortality is also rooted in "la plenitud del ser": "one cannot fall out of this field of consciousness; there are no edges of Being from which one might fall off into nothingness; in that Being you are immortal . . . " (NTV, p. 172).

Macedonio probably did not succeed in expressing all that this constellation of ideas signified to him. Adolfo de Obieta suggests this when he says regarding the final metaphysical statement his father spoke of writing, "I have the impression that he took it with him, that it cannot be found among his papers" (García, *Hablan*, p. 16).

It seems probable that Macedonio's apprehension of *la plenitud del ser* surpassed his ability to make meaningful statements about it in words. But even without fully comprehending all that this conviction meant to him, we can recognize that his experience of it as truth was critical: it shaped his life and work and was the source of his most profound ideas.

Macedonio's Idealism

Macedonio summarizes his position as follows:

> My idealism consists of three theses: . . . there only exists that which is perceived; what exists can be fully known; and the state, or Being, is selfless, for the Self would be for the state as much of an external as Matter itself. An Idealism with a subject would be dualistic. (NTV, p. 180)

"Sólo hay lo sentido"; only that which is perceived can be said to exist. An orange is a collection of sensations of color, texture, fragrance, and so on, and nothing more. There is no substance that gives rise to these sensations.

> Being, all phenomena, are states created out of nothing and incessantly extinguished into nothing. Being is full in all its states, whether of waking or dreaming, whether internal or external in appearance; nothing is a representation of something else, nothing is the appearance of something else. . . . (NTV, p. 149)

In a humorous vein he says,

> In metaphysics it is irritating that one should believe . . . that the pleasant fragrance of a flower, its color, the pliant caress of its touch do not constitute sufficient "substance." This is bad taste, the falsetto of metaphysics. ("La metafísica, Crítica del Conocimiento' la Mística, Crítica del Ser" [1924], NTV, p. 68)

The second thesis follows from the first. If the world consists only of *"estados"* ("states"), and these are not images or reflections of unknowable essences or eternal ideas, then reality itself can be properly known. However, just as the form of the flower is omitted from Macedonio's catalogue of its qualities, so is any serious consideration of what constitutes knowledge omitted from his metaphysics. The terms *state, phenomenon, sensation,* and *image* are not defined, and the essential question of how a flower is known as a flower is never dealt with. Nevertheless, there is no more frequently repeated phrase in *No toda es vigilia* than "Reality, being, is completely knowable," and in human terms Macedonio's meaning is clear enough:

Being is not plenitude if it is not fully knowable. Those who have espoused Idealism have not dug deep enough to see that unlimited knowledge was correlative to it, that there is no Idealism unless one affirms the constant substantiality of Being in each one of its states in any field of consciousness, strictly in the only field of Consciousness, which is being itself, and that this constant substantiality is fully cognizable. (NTV, p. 119)

The world, all that exists, is a series of "states" existing in consciousness. One of Macedonio's axioms is, "The world is not given." This is a way of saying that we must transcend the grammatical formulations of our own thought, which all but oblige us to conceive of a world-object given *by* a cosmic donor *to* a recipient self. Macedonio would convince us that these relationships are illusory, that they persist as vestiges of a primitive and erroneous metaphysics.

Our most fundamental assumptions concerning the relationship between mind and body are challenged by

Macedonio's view of consciousness, a view not unlike that underlying the *Upanishads*. Physical bodies, for example, do not give rise to consciousness: "your perceiving and your thinking are not located in your body, for consciousness cannot be situated anywhere; on the contrary, it is your body which exists in your mind . . . " (NTV, p. 172). Consciousness cannot be "situated" *("la sensibilidad . . . no es situable espacialmente")* (NTV, p. 173). Consciousness does not begin with birth: "Your awareness, reader, is beginningless." Nor are individual fields of consciousness absolutely separate:

> We could as well say that the one who is writing (or feels that he is writing) here is you and the one who is reading, I, for consciousness cannot be situated in a body. . . . Really, the denomination of a state as *your* state is as false, the possessive relationship is as unrepresentable as the denomination 'someone else's state.' Every state falls within a single identifying chain of consciousness. . . . (NTV, p. 173)

The struggle to clarify these ideas, and especially to resolve the contradictions inhering in the notion of a consciousness simultaneously individual and universal, fills most of the second half of *No toda es vigilia*. Macedonio's third thesis, concerning the nature of the self, is a critical one, then, and one that he has great difficulty in enunciating.

On one level, Macedonio's treatment of the subject of the self is hardly more than a recapitulation of some of the observations of Locke and Hume, with some additional insights from his own experience and from James's *Principles of Psychology*. Locke had criticized the notion of personal substances as "the principle of self-sameness in different minds." "Experientially," he says, "our personal identity consists in nothing more than the functional and perceptible fact that our later states of mind continue and remember our earlier ones."[1] Hume's essay "On Personal Identity" is probably familiar to the reader. Hume cannot discover any underlying entity he can call "self"; what he discovers, invariably, are particular perceptions or thoughts:

> For my part, when I enter most intimately into what I call *myself*, I always stumble on some particular perception or other, or heat or cold, light or shade, love or hatred, pain or pleasure. I can never catch myself at any time without a perception, and can never observe anything but the perception. When my perceptions are removed, as by sound sleep, so long am I insensible of *myself*, and may truly be said not to exist. And were all my perceptions eliminated by death and I could neither think, nor feel, nor see, nor love, nor hate after the dissolution of my body, I should be entirely annihilated, nor do I conceive what is farther requisite to make me a perfect non-entity. If anyone upon serious consideration and unprejudiced reflection thinks he has a different notion of himself, I confess I can no longer deal with him. All I can allow him is, that he may be in the right as well as I, and that we are essentially different in this particular. He may, perhaps, perceive something simple and continuous, which he calls himself; though I am certain there is no such principle in me. (*A Treatise of Human Nature*, Vol. 4)

Similarly, James tells us in *The Principles of Psychology* that his attempts to perceive a self also end in the apprehension of some particular perception:

When . . . I grapple with particulars coming to the closest possible quarters with the facts, *it is difficult for me to detect in the activity any purely spiritual element at all. Whenever my introspective glance succeeds in turning round quickly enough to catch one of these manifestations of spontaneity in the act, all it can ever feel distinctly is some bodily process, for the most part taking place within the head.* (1:Ch. 10)

Macedonio's own investigations produce similar results. He cannot discover a distinct entity he can call self:

With my intelligence as chronicler I communicate to the reader: I have encountered no Self either inside of me or outside of me; and I have noted that upon discovering in an inventory of all my perceptions that there was no Self, the "wonder of being" which had troubled me for years suddenly disappeared. (NTV, p. 179)

Virasoro, in his review of *No toda es vigilia*, summarizes Macedonio's observations regarding the self as follows:

Being, the world, all that is, is phenomenon. The internal-external state, that which is perceived. Aside from perception nothing exists. The self which perceives and the thing perceived are two abstractions, two empty hypotheses. From this point of view, the author in his denial of the subject holds to the old conception of it as substance, as abstract subject prior to knowledge, a conception which has been discarded by contemporary Idealism, which defines it as the *concrete act of knowing*. He remains in

this way somewhat out of the mainstream of modern
philosophy, taking up the problem at the precise
point at which Hume had left it upon demonstrating
that the arguments adduced by Berkeley against the
reality of the object were equally applicable to the
subject. (p. 225)

As Virasoro says, Macedonio's first concern is to deny
the self as "substance" and as "abstract subject," and he
does this in arguments not very different from Hume's. If
this demonstration were merely an academic exercise on
Macedonio's part, his observations would have little
interest for us. Macedonio, however, does not write with
Hume's detachment; his apprehension of the truth of his
discovery concerning the self is much more than an
intellectual recognition. A powerful sense of release or
liberation accompanied the experience: "Upon discovering that there was no Self . . . the 'wonder of being'
which had troubled me for years suddenly disappeared"
(NTV, p. 179).

Following James's broad definition of the term,
Macedonio calls the *experience* of this discovery as truth
"mystical." This aspect of his thought and experience
warrants careful examination.

Mystical Awareness

He who fears to nullify the Self remains in a critical
posture, having the Self before him for the last time,
and Mystical Awareness before him for the first time.
. . . (NTV, p. 152)

Throughout Macedonio's work there are repeated
references to the mystic state, many of them extremely

puzzling. The reader who is prepared to take the author at his word, and assume that what is signified is a genuine mystical experience, is struck not only by the unusual character of some of the statements but also by the extreme casualness of the author's tone. He speaks as if "La Mística" were part of everyone's common experience. It is tempting to conclude that he is using the term *mystic* in a restricted, personal sense, that he is not talking about mysticism as it is usually understood at all. I believe such a conclusion would be erroneous; yet if we take the author at his word, several important questions must be considered: just what does he mean by *La mística;* has he himself had mystical experiences?; what importance, if any, does mystical consciousness have in the evolution of his art and philosophy?

William James conceived of the mystic state as a sort of continuum embracing a very broad spectrum of experiences differing in quality and intensity. These ranged from a "sudden deepened awareness of the significance of a maxim or formula," through the sense of *déjà vu* and states of drug-altered consciousness, to the classic descriptions of religious rapture recorded by the saints *(Varieties of Religious Experience,* lectures XVI and XVII, "Mysticism"). It is very likely that Macedonio, who was familiar with *The Varieties of Religious Experience,* took James's very broad definition as his own. *Estado místico,* at any rate, seems to signify several different levels of mystical awareness, some of them *not* very far removed from our ordinary experience of reality.

Macedonio's descriptions of the mystic state comprise a kind of spectrum. Common to all these descriptions is the mention of some degree of dissolution of self-awareness. At the faint extreme of the spectrum, Macedonio, like James, mentions the experience of *déjà vu,* "perhaps the

D

threshold of mystical experience" (NTV, p. 195). Of
greater intensity are moments of complete self-absorption
in contemplation or meditation:

> At certain moments of mental plenitude, I forget
> my "self," my body, my ties, my memories, the past,
> all the acts and impressions which determined my
> sense of remoteness and the whole long trajectory
> of evasion and separation. I feel as if I have always
> been here or that my existence has just begun. But
> soon even my own existence becomes a matter which
> has not the slightest consequence for me; "time" and
> "space" are notions which have vanished; everything
> occurs without reference to place: there is no near
> nor separate nor lasting nor persisting nor before nor
> after. ("Bases en Metafísica" [1908]. NTV, p. 15)

When more fully developed, *el estado místico* appears to
be a return to the state of prereflective innocence, a
return, in other words, to a kind of undifferentiated
awareness in which there is as yet no distinction between
subject and object: "[return] to the mystic state, to the
existence of a child before he has begun to reflect in
terms of subject and object. . . . The same state in which
animals and premetaphysical man exist . . ." ("Descripcio-
metafísica" [1942], NTV, p. 191).

This awareness brings with it the sense of oneness of
which mystics of every persuasion give testimony. For
Macedonio this sense seems not so much to contain the
metaphysical answer as to *be* the answer. A metaphysical
enigma is a pseudo-problem, "a mishap of the mind
which is remedied by the conscious dissolution of all the
so-called principles of thought, of reason, of substance, of
the identity of consciousness, of historical identity or of

the world" ("Descripcio-metafísica," NTV, p. 191). For this reason Macedonio insists that metaphysics cannot make use of *a priori* methods in order to dispel *el asombro de ser,* "to show us the way to regain that familiarity."

The familiarity Macedonio is referring to can only be regained through the kind of experience we have been describing: "He who fears to nullify the Self remains in a critical posture, having the Self before him for the last time and Mystical Awareness before him for the first time . . ." (NTV, p. 152). For this reason, we have suggested that the aim of his metaphysics is not an explanation of the nature of ultimate reality but an experience of it, an experience that must be, finally, nonsensuous and non-intellective.

If we are careful to distinguish between mystical experience and its interpretation by the mystic himself, we can see that the experience, which is probably universal,* can be clothed in a great variety of garb, usually, though not always, the symbology of a given religion. A large group of mystics, however, interprets the experience in nontheistic language, as Zaehner points out in his well-known study, *Mysticism Sacred and Profane.* Thus Tennyson

---

*I am aware that many eminent commentators take exception to this view. R. C. Zaehner, for example, in his excellent book *Mysticism Sacred and Profane,* takes the position that there is a qualitative difference in mystic experiences that ought not to be glossed over lightly. "To assert that all mystics speak the same language and convey the same message does not seem to hold true even within one particular religious tradition" (p. 27), he insists. James, however, emphasizes the universal character of mystic experience and admits as mystic a great variety of states of consciousness, as we have noted. He does not distinguish sharply between religious and secular mystic *experience,* nor would Macedonio, in my opinion.

speaks of "boundless being"; the German philosopher Karl Joel describes a moment when "within and without are one."† Arthur Koestler speaks of "floating on a river of peace, under bridges of silence," and of reaching a point at which "there was no river and no I" (quoted in Walter T. Stace, *The Teachings of the Mystics*, p. 233).

Similarly, Macedonio's interpretation of *el estado místico* makes no use of the terms of conventional religious language. There is no reference either to God or to a universal absolute. In fact, he tells us that in the mystic state there *is* no notion of subordination to a Creator ("Descripcio-metafísica," NTV, p. 190). His interpretation of the mystic state is nearly "naked." For the most part his language is nonemotive and matter-of-fact, certainly not "lyrical, and sweet, and universal as the rising of the wind," as Emerson tells us the speech of a mystic must be.* The starkness of his language and his dispassionate, impersonal tone make it difficult to believe that these are his own experiences that he is describing; yet, if they are not, certain of his insights are very difficult to account for.

In Western tradition, mysticism, even in its secular forms, usually signifies a unitive experience of some kind. Religious mystics speak of union with a divine being, and secular mystics speak of union with some natural principle or force. Macedonio avoids the duality of such a formulation. In one of the most fully developed descriptions he gives us of the mystic state, published in the last decade of

† Tennyson and Joel are both discussed in *Mysticism Sacred and Profane*.

*An exception must be made of the arresting metaphors of his "Poema de trabajos de estudios de las estéticas de la siesta" (PR66, pp. 272–76): ". . . quietud y visión hacen del Todo un ¡ah!, el elevarse de un ¡ah!"

his life, he refers to a reach of consciousness beyond the very notion of oneness:

> The mystic state is living without a notion of one's beginning, without a notion of cessation, without a notion of individual history, without a notion of personal identity, without a notion of the identity or recognizability of the cosmos, without a notion of the unity of the cosmos, without a notion of personal unity, without sense of movement in any direction nor any silhouette of unity, without a notion of subordination to a Creator. The mystical state is living as if uncreated and self-subsistent; and I believe that it is also living without discriminating between image and perception, dream and reality, and without distinguishing between the newly remembered and the already familiar dream. ("Descripcio-Metafísica," NTV, p. 190)

Macedonio describes here a state of awareness beyond all concepts, including that of oneness.

This idea is not frequent in Western mysticism. It is characteristic, of course, of the mysticism of certain Eastern religions. "Mystics of Hindu and Buddhist cultures, as well as Plotinus and many others . . . insist that it is incorrect to speak of a mystical experience as an apprehension of the Unity (since this supposes a separation between subject and object). We should rather say that the experience *is* the One. Christianity, Judaism and Islam, which consider it heretical or blasphemous for the creature to claim identity with the creator, normally speak dualistically of 'union' with the Creator" (Stace, *Teachings,* p. 238). The experience, then, is not "unitive" in the sense that the self becomes one with the divine being or some element in nature, for such formulations imply a previous disassociation that is rendered whole.* The experience seems to be one of sensing an ever-present wholeness in which all concepts, including that of wholeness, cease to exist. In Hindu terms, *atman* knows itself as *Brahman.*

Understood as the description of the experience of enlightenment, the last-quoted passage is more comprehensible. *"Vivir sin noción de identidad personal,"* and so forth, could mean to live in the world having "seen through" it, to live in a world in which, though nothing has changed, everything has changed. "Shut your eyes and change to and wake another way of seeing, which everyone has but few use," Plotinus tells us (Stace, *Teachings,* p. 114).

Walter T. Stace makes an important observation about the relation between a mystical idea and a mystical experience:

> [Mystical idea] means an idea, belief, opinion or proposition which was originally based on mystical experience, although the connection between the experience and the opinion may have been quite forgotten. The point is that a mystical idea is the product of the conceptual intellect, whereas a mystical experience is a nonintellectual mode of consciousness. The proposition that "time is unreal" is an example of a mystical idea. It must have arisen because mystics usually feel that (a) their experience is timeless

---

*Thus Plotinus writes, "We should not speak of seeing, but, instead of seen and seer, speak boldly of a simple unity, for in this seeing we neither distinguish nor are there two" (Stace, *Teachings,* p. 15).

and (b) it is more real (in some sense) than any other experience. . . . A mystical idea may be true or false, but it must have originated in a genuine mystical experience. (p. 10)

It would appear that some of Macedonio's principal ideas originated as Stace describes; the constellation of ideas surrounding *"El ser es siempre pleno,"* for example, may have had such an origin. One reason for believing this is Macedonio's constant, and not entirely successful, struggle with language. *No toda es vigilia* is strewn with the wreckage of linguistic battles in which the seer was defeated by an intransigent syntax. The ideas he wants to express are notoriously difficult to put into words, and many of his statements have the look of desperate solutions:

The mystic state . . . is to live as if uncreated and self-subsistent" ("Descripcio-Metafísica," NTV, p. 191).

We are experience. We occur our states (NTV, p. 154).

. . . that a self, which cannot be anything but a my-self, in short, I, should occur to being; that to happening, to the "changes," there should occur a self; that Being should always self-occur, self-be, is the Mystery (NTV, p. 152).

I call being a selfless psychic phenomenon (NTV, p. 87).

Much of what is baffling and exasperating in *No toda es*

vigilia la de los ojos abiertos may be the result of the phenomenon described by Stace, i.e., "the connection between
the experience and the opinion may [be] quite forgotten."
The contradictions and non sequiturs, the jerry-built
arguments and dogmatic pronouncements may reflect this
process. Certainly the entire text is an agonized attempt
to force language to transcend its natural limitations. At
his most pessimistic, Macedonio says that he thinks he
may be writing only for himself (an idea he expresses
with some frequency):

> The word is not necessary to that which is called
> thought. Thought or Intelligence adds nothing to the
> manifestation of being, and therefore it is nothing
> more than a record of what we call the past. Being,
> phenomenism, has no law. There exist no laws nor
> principles of logic or reason which can control being.
> What I have just stated about the word being a sign
> evoking the past might simply cease to occur . . .
> and I may, therefore, be writing in vain, for myself
> alone. (NTV, p. 148)

Macedonio's struggle with language is the inevitable
concomitant of his rejection of Western conceptions of
reality. As is apparent by now, Macedonio's world view
was much closer to that of the East than to that of the
West. A close parallel to Macedonio's monistic idealism
can be found, for example, in the teaching of the Hindu
philosopher Sankara.* And Alicia Jurado, the first

*I am indebted for this comparison to Adolfo de Obieta.
Obieta has not developed in writing the parallel to be found
between his father's system and that of the eighth-century Hindu
teacher, but in the prologue to *No toda es vigilia* (Centro Editor

commentator, to my knowledge, to note the Eastern flavor of certain of Macedonio's statements, has found similarities between his formulations and the teachings of Mahayana Buddhism ("Aproximación a Macedonio Fernández").

We can only speculate why Macedonio's meditations led him in this direction. It is very unlikely that he had any special knowledge of Eastern texts, although his thorough familiarity with the work of Schopenhauer, with its wealth of Buddhist and Hindu references, may well have been an important factor. In fact, there are clear indications of Schopenhauer's influence at key points in the text: "Consciousness is one and therefore not subject to numerality; it cannot really be labeled 'one.' Individual means 'memorious,' since the form of individuation is illusory (Schopenhauer)" (NTV, p. 89).

Hume may have been another influence in this process, strangely enough. Hume's denial of the reality of the self, which Macedonio endorsed, is actually stated in arguments not very different from those attributed to the Buddha (Stace, *Teachings,* p. 238). Macedonio's apprehension of that idea, however, was not merely intellectual, as was Hume's. Macedonio seems to have experienced the idea as truth in what a theologian might call a religious encounter, or in what he himself might call *el estado místico.*

---

edition), he muses that it would be an interesting project to prepare a special edition of NTV which would point out the affinity of certain of his father's theses (the denial of the self, for example) and those of Sankara. Readers wishing to pursue this comparison will find a concise account of Sankara's teaching in *Philosophers Speak of God* by Charles Hartshorne and William L. Reese (Chicago: University of Chicago Press, 1953).

Dreams

As a corollary to his belief that "being is always full in all its states," Macedonio was prepared to go to extremes to affirm the parity of all experiences of the mind. The events of *ensueño* and *vigilia* are equally real in consciousness; "no toda es vigilia la de los ojos abiertos": waking consciousness does not exhaust the possibilities of valid experience of reality. The experiences of the mind cannot be hierarchized: "Dreams and reality are not degrees of consciousness, for being manifests itself with the same plenitude in all its states; existence is equally substantial in all of them . . ." (NTV, p. 114).

The dream state interests Macedonio precisely because, like the mystic state, it is immediate in consciousness. As mystic perception occurs in the eternal now (*un solo hoy*), the mode of dream consciousness is always "the present indicative."[2] Dreaming, for its immediacy in consciousness, was for Macedonio "the true mode of being": "Being *is* because it is a Dream, that is, a plenitude which is immediate. Being would be nothing if it were not immediate to the soul as the Dream state is, if it were like Matter and the Self, not perceived but inferred . . ." (NTV, p. 87).

If all of life were experienced with the immediacy of a dream, all would be well. There would be no *wonder of being*; metaphysics would be superfluous. We would know reality directly, "in the style of a dream":

> The style of a dream is the only possible form of Being, its only conceivable form. By "style of a dream" I mean everything which is presented in its entirety as a state of subjective awareness, without pretensions of external correlations. . . . (NTV, p. 87)

Like the surrealists, Macedonio is eager to erode the inordinate prestige of waking consciousness:

Vigilia, you are not everything;
   there is a deeper awakening: mystic awareness.
And dreams behind closed eyelids.

(NTV, p. 75)

Erroneously, we identify *vigilia* ("waking consciousness") with *"la famosa realidad"*; "let reality be that which is questioned," Macedonio insists. His challenge to the primacy of *vigilia* parallels that of the surrealists, and certain of his exhortations recall those of André Breton in *Les vases communicants* and elsewhere. However, Macedonio's conception of dreams and their relationship to art was very different from that of the surrealists. The surrealists held that dreaming and waking consciousness existed in a state of tension that, according to their dialectic, could give rise to a new level of consciousness over and above our normal perception of reality: the fecund world of symbol and imagery that the surrealist artist exploited in his works. For Macedonio the kind of synthesis the surrealists spoke of was inconceivable. As must be evident by now, thinking in terms of thesis and antithesis was a habit of mind entirely alien to him; waking and dreaming were in his view completely fluid states between which there is no tension. Consequently, the surrealists' enthusiasm for recording the images of dream and delirium was incomprehensible to Macedonio; recording such images was a mere copying that certainly did not qualify as art: "To copy, to narrate fantasies, even dreams and nightmares, is not art: there are a million nightmares in every human head and were they all exposed in print, they would not have the slightest

interest . . ." ("Sobre 'Belarte,' poesía o prosa," *Poesía*
1:43).

Macedonio, then, is not interested in dream images per
se; he cares little for the psychoanalytic, mythological, or
aesthetic possibilities of dream imagery. As for the metaphysical difficulties presented by his Idealism, Macedonio
actually says little about dreams that had not already been
said by Kant, Hobbes, Schopenhauer, or Hume. His long,
pseudoscientific analysis of the difference between *vigilia*
and *ensueño* is ingenuous and rather tedious, revealing at
last only one "insignificant" difference between the two
states: the events of *vigilia* produce effects; those of
ensueño do not. The flames of *ensueño* do not burn the
flesh; the flames of *vigilia* do: "If one is not concerned
about effects, there is no difference between what happens
and what we imagine." If it were not for this curious
difference, the two states would be identical, for "they fill
our time with equal efficacy."

Here the motive of the long disquisition on dreams at
last becomes apparent. Borges in "Nueva refutación del
tiempo" ("New Refutation of Time") demonstrated the
efficacy of the experience of "two identical moments" in
triggering an intuition of the meaning of the word
eternity[3]; Macedonio discerns a similar potential in another
type of looking-glass experience: the experience of an
event whose effects are so nearly imperceptible as to make
it impossible to determine whether it was dreamed or real.
Macedonio finds such an event in the fifth chapter of
The World as Will and Representation.

Here Schopenhauer recalls Hobbes's observation that we
easily mistake dreams for reality when we have unin-
tentionally fallen asleep in our clothes. "In these cases
waking is almost as little observed as falling asleep;

dream and reality flow into each other and become confused." "Life and dreams," Schopenhauer continues in the familiar passage, "are leaves of one and the same book. The systematic reading is real life: . . . our idle thumbing through the pages when the reading hour (the day) has come to an end . . . is called dreaming." Macedonio ruffles these pages to produce a memorable scene: we see the philosopher Hobbes, who has fallen sleep in his chair, awaken in a hotel room in twentieth-century Buenos Aires. Here, not sure whether he is awake or asleep, he is privileged to discuss metaphysics with "el metafísico del barrio," Macedonio Fernández.

Those moments in which "dream and reality flow together and become confused" are a privileged point in consciousness: at such moments we intimate that the life of the mind is eternal; "though we never wake again, we shall never lack a single image": "the Affection reveals itself as the direct creator of the world of the images it is pleased to create; although the other world, Reality, never returned, that is to say, even though we were never to awake again, . . . we should never lack a single image" (NTV, p. 169). In death, the thumbing through the pages we have called Waking or Dreaming continues uninterrupted; the leaves of the book are infinite.

Muerte es Beldad

Dreaming, for Macedonio, says Adolfo de Obieta, is not an interruption of reality, but a deeper experience of it; death, by analogy, is not a cessation of consciousness, but a shift to a deeper form of awareness. In Obieta's words,

Metaphysically speaking, he does not make a distinction in his conceptions between dream and reality. His purpose is not to distinguish waking

consciousness from dreaming. . . . He did not believe
that dreaming was an interruption of reality, but a
more profound experience of it. It seemed to him
that the individual during those moments of dreaming
lived very intensely and had as many experiences or
more than he had with his eyes open while he was
awake.

. . . Just as he did not concede more importance to
the waking state than to the dream state, neither did
he concede more importance to the state of life than to
the supposed state of death, because every state was
essentially the same: death, dream, waking, all of these
were *liveable*. (García, *Hablan,* pp. 21–22)

We have suggested that Macedonio's view of consciousness is Vedantic in nature. "Death is fictitious
because *birth* is a fiction, . . ." Macedonio wrote to
Ricardo Victorica after the death of Elena. We cannot
affirm that consciousness is endless without also affirming
that it is beginningless, he suggests. "From this gateway
Moment a long eternal lane runs *back*; an eternity lies
behind us," Nietzsche wrote in *Thus Spake Zarathustra.*
Life before birth has rarely been a subject of serious
concern in Western tradition, and yet an eternal existence
beginning with physical birth, as conceived in Christian
philosophy, is hardly logical, as Schopenhauer demon-
strates in his essay on death: "Whoever regards the
birth of man as his absolute beginning must also regard
death as his absolute end" (*World as Will and Representation,* supplements, ch. 16). Macedonio, who had drunk
deep of the great essay on death, urges us to consider this
idea, for it is essential to our full understanding of *la
plenitud del ser*: "Your consciousness, reader, is *beginningless.*" Birth is not our beginning; death is not our end; it

is impossible for the individual to "fall out of being": "one cannot fall out of this field of consciousness; there are no edges of Being from which one might fall off into nothingness; in that Being you are immortal . . ." (NTV, p. 172).

Schopenhauer had also insisted that the individual "falls back always into the lap of nature." But Macedonio was not thinking, as Schopenhauer was, of a grinding round of rebirth. Macedonio did not believe that "we are something that never should have been," "an error which ought not to be perpetuated." His reverence for life and his belief in the transcendence of love transform and humanize Schopenhauer's grim answer to the question of immortality. Those who prize life highly find little consolation in Schopenhauer's version of eternal existence; there is small solace in being told that "the rainbow on the waterfall is constant, though the individual drops are cast and recast into the void," when it is precisely the destiny of the individual drops that interests us. Macedonio never speaks with such monstrous detachment; his doctrine of immortality is invariably illumined by a word that is a four-syllable guarantee of grace: what awaits us after death is "eternidad *nemónica*," ("*memorious* eternity"). His is no doctrine of the indestructibility of matter nor of the persistence of undifferentiated psychic energy; we are to have eternal *memory* of ourselves as individuals:

Plainer than Day
   is Being,
the fullness of our being,
everlasting,
individual and memorious,
without beginning, without break, without end.
                                        (NTV, p. 75)

Consciousness, then, does not originate with birth, nor is it linked to the fate of the body. The body is merely an intermediary; it does not possess consciousness, for consciousness cannot be situated in space.

Like the disappearance of the stars at dawn, death is an illusion, *una ocultación*. The body vanishes, but the person endures. "We only know the death and birth of bodies, not of persons" (NTV, p. 182). The spirit, not being linked to the destiny of the body, persists in death in another mode of consciousness. "Our eternity, an infinite dreaming exactly like the present, is absolutely certain" (M, p. 27).

An Aesthetics of Challenge

If the *Weltanschauung* of the Western world deeply distressed Macedonio, so, inevitably, did its system of literature. As he is moved to contest the metaphysical notions he believed injurious, so also will he contest the aesthetic principles these have given rise to. He contests these principles both in theory and in practice, both in his theory of literature, which we are about to examine, and in his works of fiction, especially his novel, *Museo de la novela de la Eterna*.

As we have noted, Macedonio challenged the assumption that behind the phenomenal world there lies another, more real realm, variously named in the history of Western philosophy. Accordingly, his literary theory contested a universal principle of Western literature, the principle of verisimilitude, based as it is upon the unspoken assumption that there is behind every fictional world a world more real, more authoritative than itself. Macedonio, violently rejecting a literature of "copies," will espouse an aesthetic of "nonrealism."

Macedonio contests the notion that the world is "given," presumably by a cosmic donor who definitively fashioned it for a passive recipient, man. Accordingly, he will contest the conventional literary circuit that reiterates this notion—author/book/reader—casting doubt upon the fundamental concept of the "work" of literature. Macedonio rejects the notions that consciousness is "divisible," that it is "situated" in a physical body whose destiny it shares and that there is an entity called *self* existing above and beyond experience. Conventional theories of characterization are of course brought into question by his views, and he will use the literary personage and the author-reader relation as means of affirming his own conception of consciousness.

Macedonio, as we have observed, insists upon the parity of all psychic states; he contests our tendency to gradate these states according to their relative "reality." In his novel, Macedonio will work to erode the boundaries that customarily separate dreaming and waking, life and art, literature and reality, insisting that fiction, "the self-authenticating dream of art," is as real as any other experience of life.

Chapter III

Theory of the Novel:
Belarte Conciencial

Ian Watt and others have shown how closely the rise of the modern novel is linked to the rise of philosophic Realism.[1] The development of the novel seems to have paralleled the process whereby the insights of Realist philosophers imperceptibly became part of the common view of reality of the common man. The type of novel that arose in this tradition has enjoyed such extraordinary success, expressing so satisfactorily our common view of the world, that it is even now practically synonymous with what we mean when we say "novel."

What Macedonio calls "novel" is the antithesis of the traditional novel, opposing it at every critical point. His literary theory calls into question every aspect of its conception, content, execution, and function. In *Museo* every narrative procedure that might contribute to the development of a novel is systematically avoided: the idea of authorship is undermined as well as the principles

97

of coherent development; the very concept of "beginning" and "ending" is nullified. But *Museo* is not the result of an arbitrary attempt to write a novel resembling a novel as little as possible, to paraphrase Ortega's famous formula. *Museo* is, like the traditional novel, a product of the philosophical milieu in which it was conceived. If the novelistic world of Fielding and Richardson epitomized the philosophical world of Mill and Locke, Macedonio's *Museo* epitomizes the dynamic world of his own philosophic Idealism.

Macedonio's metaphysical texts, as we have seen, were combative, aggressively challenging our common assumptions concerning reality. The text he calls "novel" — and persists in calling "novel," since he has no other name for it—is equally combative. It is conceived, in fact, as a deliberate "provocation to the Realist school" (M, p. 38). But far more is challenged by *Museo* than the principles of Realism. "Realist school," for Macedonio, as we shall see, encompasses very nearly the entire body of Western literature. Noé Jitrik, in his seminal study of *Museo* ("La 'futura novela' de Macedonio Fernández"), has demonstrated that what ultimately comes into crisis in Macedonio's "novel" is nothing less than the Western concept of the "work" of art, the solid, static, well-defined product of an individual author.

The work of art is assaulted by Macedonio for reasons that have more to do with his metaphysics than with the literary experimentation of the avant-garde. The image of the work is challenged by Macedonio's aesthetics, we should like to suggest, as a surrogate for the image of the world challenged by his metaphysics. As commonly conceived, world and work, great orb and small, were images incapable of signifying Macedonio's conception of reality. His metaphysics opposed to the solid material "world" a reality conceived as a dynamic flux of mental "states" incessantly rising and falling; his aesthetics opposed to the "work" of literature a "novel" whose text aspired to something of the same fluidity.

Macedonio's alternative to the literary work is the problematical "text-in-the-making," to use Noé Jitrik's invaluable term. For Macedonio, all previous literature had been the product of the principle of verisimilitude. The "novel" he envisioned was to be a product not of verisimilitude, but of what he called "nonrealism." All of the techniques of nonrealism serve to ensure the dynamism of the text-in-the-making, primarily by thwarting in some way the development of a closed or finished work. The "open" structure of this text, the permutability of its elements, and its infinite digressions operate to prevent the "novel" from "crystallizing," as Jitrik puts it, from developing into a novel, a "work" of literature.

The text-in-the-making is a complex concept having many disquieting aspects. It challenges the principles of causality, coherence, and unity that we normally consider the basis of narration, since in opposing the novel, the "novel" must defeat at all cost the process of development that characterizes it. The author/work/reader circuit is constantly interrupted for the same reason. In addition, the "novel" aspires to induce in the reader a kind of "ontological shock," a revelatory flash of intuition, perhaps mystical in nature, that Macedonio calls a "disruption of the certainty of being" (*la conmoción de la certeza del ser*). As if this did not present sufficient difficulty, the concept of the text-in-the-making is revealed to us in *Museo* indirectly, through a long series of negations; we must gradually infer what the "novel" *is* on the basis of what we are told it is *not*. Adding to the complexity is the fact that we are dealing with a great comic text. The confusions, ambiguities, and ironies surrounding the sabotage of the traditional novel provide a lush field for Macedonian humor, and we must constantly make allowances for comic exaggeration in our apprehension of the "novel."

No single, organic statement of Macedonio's literary theory exists. The aesthetics of Idealism, however, interested him mightily, and his letters and journals contain many references to the theory of "Belarte conciencial," as he called it. In addition, there are several published pieces that are useful in reconstructing his theory, including "Doctrina estética de la novela," first given as a radio broadcast in 1929, and "Para una teoría de la humorística," a long and scholarly article containing valuable comments on Belarte.[2] By far the most important source, however, is *Museo* itself. For one thing, the numerous "prologues" to the "novel" contain explicit lessons in aesthetic theory for characters and readers. More importantly, the whole novelistic venture is conceived as an inquiry into the nature of novel writing; the course of the "novel" and its theoretical basis are constantly contested by all concerned. Literary theory, in fact, has such preponderance in *Museo* that Macedonio is moved to remark, "If what I call novel fails as such, my Aesthetic Theory will save the day: I am, willing for *it* to be taken as a novel, as first-rate fantasy, as a stand-in for the novel. If the novel fails as such, it may be that my Aesthetics will serve as a good novel" (M, p. 40).

Born of Macedonio's Idealism, the theory of Belarte Conciencial is the articulation between *No toda es vigilia la de los ojos abiertos* and *Museo de la novela de la Eterna*. The more clearly Macedonio discerned alternatives to prevailing notions of reality, the more deeply he was convinced that these notions constituted an inadequate and crippling world view. One of his motives in writing *No toda es vigilia* was "to liberate human thought"—to shatter this image of the world and project an alternative. The object of *Museo* is very similar: to shatter the image of the work—which is the recapitulation of this world view—and to propose an alternative. The theory of Belarte Conciencial is the strategy for carrying out this radical program.

Macedonio announces his intention quietly enough at the beginning of *Museo*: "The present aesthetic project is a provocation to the realist school, a program of total discreditation of the truth or reality of what the novel relates, a complete surrender to the truth of Art—intrinsic, unconditional, and self-authenticating . . ." (M, p. 38).

The "challenge to the realist school" and the projection of an alternative to its product are the basis both of the humor and the philosophic content of *Museo*. On one level, *Museo* is a parody of novel writing in which the novel's precarious existence is ironically undercut by the author in every conceivable way, providing endless comic possibilities. But the assault upon the traditional novel is also an assault upon the "world" that gave rise to it. If in *Museo* Macedonio produced "the most experimental book to date," as Rodríguez Monegal suggests,[3] if Macedonio's theory of literature is ultimately more radical than that of any of his avant-garde disciples, it is because his assault is launched not against mere literary conventions but against the unspoken assumptions that underlie them; Macedonio challenges nothing less than the fundamental principles that govern life and thought in the Western world.

It is important that we keep in mind the philosophical context of Macedonio's assault upon the novel. If we do not, we might hastily conclude that *Museo* is simply a literary curiosity, an eccentric example of hyperaestheticism bearing no relation to fundamental human concerns. *Museo,* is, in fact, like *No toda es vigilia,* deeply committed to "the liberation of human thought." The attack upon traditional narrative structure really is a heroic assault upon metaphysical notions Macedonio considered repressive of the free and eternal life of the spirit.

It is no coincidence that Macedonio's theory of art first came to light during the perfervid period of avant-garde activity in the 1920s. Although he was born in 1874, the same year as Lugones, Macedonio had played no part in the development of Argentine Modernism. With the exception of two poems, Macedonio, contemptuous of the literature of "pretty sounds" (*soniditos*), published nothing until the trajectory of Modernism was complete. When Borges returned to Argentina in 1921, several things happened: Ultraism took root in Argentina; Borges met Macedonio, an encounter that had important consequences for both of them; and Macedonio, through Borges, at last came into contact with the mainstream of Argentine literary life. Most important of all, an intellectual atmosphere was gradually created that favored the expression of the most radical aesthetic creeds.

Macedonio's contact with the young avant-garde poets was mutually stimulating. On the basis of some early poems, he was hailed by the Ultraists as their precursor. César Fernández Moreno calls him aptly "a born writer of the avant-garde. . . . A new arrival upon the literary scene, Macedonio or Recienvenido at last found, without seeking it, his proper role when it became obvious that he was, and always had been, a member of the avant-garde, even before it existed."[4] If the Ultraists gained much from Macedonio's Socratic tertulias, Macedonio gained as well. For in the intense debates of aesthetic principles that characterized their conversations, Macedonio at last found the proper forum for the expression of his radical theories of literature.

Though its origins are different, Macedonio's theory of Belarte coincides with certain tenets of Ultraism. The Ultraists pursued an elusive ideal: poetry reduced to its purest form, independent of any extrinsic force or influence. César Fernández Moreno calls attention to what he terms the Ultraists' "aspiration for nudity" (*objetivo deseo de desnudez*).

> Ultraism was looking for a poetry even simpler than of *sencillismo*: through an even greater suppression of formal features and through an almost exclusive dependence upon image, it sought by following the eliminatory path which Valéry describes to reach a poetry reduced to its own essence, pure poetry. (*La realidad y los papeles,* p. 148)

Macedonio's aspiration for the novel parallels the Ultraist desire for purity in poetry. The novel of Belarte, he wrote to poet Pedro Juan Vignale, must contain (1) no attempt to instruct or to inform, (2) no appeal to the senses, and (3) no finality except to be itself ("Sobre 'Belarte,' " p. 43). For his own reasons Macedonio followed Valéry's "eliminatory path" to the very end. His letter to Vignale closes with the following question:

> What then is left for prose once one suppresses narrative, description, the famous *characters,* sonority, phonetic imitations, doctrines and theses (while there is science), preaching, propaganda, wise judgments, and the whole genre of sensory appeal?

His enigmatic answer was: "There remains that which can only be obtained with the written word."

In demanding "that which can only be obtained with the written word," a rigorously *literary* literature, in rejecting traditional content and insisting upon nearly impossible standards of purity, Macedonio coincided with many avant-garde theorists. But even in aspiring to the ideal of completely pure, self-subsistent creations, these writers were still committed to the concept of the work of art and to the general system of literature of which the work is a meaningful part. Macedonio's more radical repudiation of the system itself sets him even beyond the avant-garde in his aspirations.

His contact with avant-garde theorists, however, seems to have been a critical factor in bringing his own aesthetic theory to light. The fact that his silence remained nearly unbroken until he was almost fifty years old seems to suggest that before the decline of Modernism, an atmosphere favoring the expression of his ideas did not exist. With the advent of avant-garde activity in the 1920s, however, Macedonio seems to have felt that he could at least begin to speak of the concept of art that he envisioned with some hope of being understood. But had no one in Argentina ever heard of Cubism, Ultraism, or Creationism, Macedonio's theory of art would have been much the same, for its essential features are implicit in his metaphysics.

Macedonio's Idealism viewed reality as a dynamic flux of mental "states." The theory of Belarte embodies this view of reality; its deprecation of the material world, its aspiration for dynamism, its rejection of mimesis, its preference for the conceptual or evocative over the merely sensual—all are elements deriving from Macedonio's Idealismo Absoluto.

In *No toda es vigilia* Macedonio had worked to attenuate the difference between image and sensation, contriving to reveal the two as virtually indistinguishable. This parity between image and sensation, as César Fernández Moreno observes, becomes the basis for a kind of Creationism:

> Macedonio's Absolute Idealism solved the most pressing problem of the avant-garde with its insistence that being is solely and exclusively perceptual awareness, in the forms of both dreaming and waking, which allows a final identification of these two traditionally antithetical terms, the very conciliation of opposites which the surrealists were striving for. The underlying unity of the avant-garde could be sustained on this basis despite its various postures of extreme individualism. This individualism can be explained historically and psychologically as the withdrawal of the individual into himself as a result of the absolute failure of everything outside of him. But if reality existed in my own perceptual awareness, there was nothing strange in attempting a kind of literary creation which admitted no law other than that of my own supremely sovereign will.

Not only in underlying theory but also in the question of form, Macedonio turned out to be the the perfect teacher of Ultraism. On purely linguistic grounds, the avant-garde continually debated the possibility of creating an art independent of life; the representative nature of language constantly sent it back to life. But in Macedonio's metaphysics the problem finds an answer: if dreaming and waking are on a par, it is not obligatory "to require that every image be the result of a perception or sensation and there is no reason why absolute creation (*invención absoluta*) should not be perfectly possible." Here we have the only viable basis for any kind of *creacionismo*: the poet must invent reality no longer in the linguistic realm but in the ontic; supposing this possible, the problem of giving written form to such creation is now a purely literary one and perhaps even capable of solution; of course Macedonio himself, returning to the linguistic zone, admits that "a strictly Idealist language is not as yet available." (*La realidad y los papeles*, p. 153)

In a humorous passage in *Museo* the metaphysical basis of artistic creation is hotly debated by author, reader, and characters. The author, affirming his power as absolute creator, exclaims: "What power I have to create the appearance of life and death, to control all of this!" The character called el Metafísico then observes:

> This is a very intricate phantasmagoria of characters, readers, and author. It is not that they are merely pretending to be embroiled; they really do not know what they are. It can be resolved this way: they are all real; every image in a mind is reality and is alive; the world, all reality is merely an image in a mind . . . more than an image in a mind we cannot be . . . . . appearing in a mind is being born. (M, p. 186)

Image and sensation being equally real in the mind, the ideal of absolute creation is a theoretical possibility; but Macedonio pushes further: the image of art not only need not have a correlative in the sensible world, it *must* not have such a correlative: "Art is either superfluous, or it has nothing to do with Reality. Only in the latter case is it real, just as the elements of reality are not copies of anything else" (M, p. 109).

Art is real, that is, *art*, to the extent that it is not a copy, not a reflection of the sensible world. We recall Macedonio's attack on Kantian metaphysics in *No toda es vigilia*, which began with the heated declaration, "The present publication is inspired mainly by a desire to present a protest against 'noumenism' " (NTV, p. 85). *Museo* begins with a parallel declaration: "The present aesthetic project is a provocation to the realist school, a program of total discreditation of the truth or reality of what the novel relates, a complete surrender to the truth of Art—intrinsic, unconditional, and self-authenticicating . . . " (M, p. 38).

In Macedonio's view, realistic art, like Kantian metaphysics, denied the primacy of experience. As the phenomenal world in Kant's system points beyond itself to a more real noumenal realm, the realistic work of art, however stylized or expressive, points beyond the aesthetic experience itself to a more real model. "The noumenists concede us a life of shadows," Macedonio had said disdainfully in *No toda es vigilia*. His rejection of realistic art in *Museo* parallels this. Realism, for all its insistence on authenticity, is a play of shadows, loathsome copies of real objects. Only genuinely "artistic" art, deliberately conceived as art and not the product of verisimilitude, has real and not illusory aesthetic existence.

Macedonio's undiscriminating antagonism for representational art recalls, both for its vehemence and its seeming arbitrariness, Plato's scorn for painting and for "imitative" poetry. The antagonism of both Plato and Macedonio toward representation is fully understandable —from entirely different points of view—in the light of their deep veneration of the real. For both philosophers the cardinal sin, beside which all other merits or failings are inconsequential, lies in opting for a copy when the real is at hand. For Macedonio as well as for Plato, all arguments in defense of realistic art are entirely beside the point; all representation is essentially a copy, and *ipso facto* an abomination: "The true-to-life, the copy, is my abomination" (M, p. 41).

The famous maxim of Tlön, "Mirrors and copulation are abominable because they multiply the number of men," inevitably comes to mind. This misanthropic dictum rejects not the copy but the model. In contrast, representational art is rejected by Macedonio, as by Plato, not because it is a copy of *life*, but because it is a *copy* of life. It is not the portrayal of natural forms that repels Macedonio; it is that they are inadequately and superfluously portrayed.

If Macedonio aspires to an art that has "nothing to do with reality," it is not because of the paucity of life but because of its plenitude. Life is rich and complex, excellent beyond comparison, and utterly sufficient unto itself. "The truth of Art—intrinsic, unconditional, and self-authenticating" is not subordinate to the truth of life, nor does it pretend to supplant it.

The retreat of the avant-garde from representational art, its rejection of human content, was often motivated by a radical dissatisfaction with the day-to-day experience of life. Jorge Mañach, describing the attitudes that gave rise to Pure Poetry, recalls,

What surrounded us in life was so sordid, so mediocre, and apparently so incapable of being remedied that we sought our spiritual redemption by rising to the plane of the ideal . . . . In the avant-garde we were attempting an art completely divorced from the

almost uninhabitable world. And that is why what
came from us was that colorless and nearly substance-
less art, simultaneously soothing and stimulating, a
volatile art which evaporated upon the slightest
contact with the human atmosphere.[5]

Macedonio's rejection of the portrayal of life experience
in fiction has quite different origins; it derives, in fact,
from a surplus of faith in life. In a letter to Gómez de la
Serna he expressed his rare belief that life can be, and
frequently is, *perfect*. "My daughter Elena is perfect, my
young sons are perfect as are many children, many men,
many friends, many matrons; the dogma that there is no
perfection is a bit of hollow rhetoric."
Art cannot compete with life, nor should it attempt to.

Invented episodes are innocuous games compared
to the richness of daily life; and the effort to *communicate* emotions by trying to touch someone's
heart through realistic expositions and combinations
of words is woefully inefficient compared to the spontaneous resources of gestures, movements, and the
varied accents of an impassioned conversation. ("Doctrina estética de la novela," p. 413).

Beauty in art is not a function of beauty in life; the
two are not in the same plane. In a letter to Pedro Juan
Vignale, Macedonio remarks that he does not believe that
there is such a thing as "natural" beauty; the appeal of
child, lake, or meadow is invariably "teleological,"
serving the ends of life; *beautiful* can only be that which
is produced by art: "Beauty only exists through indirect
expression, and this expression is increasingly artistic as
it is less direct, less realistic, less a copy, less informative"
("Sobre 'Belarte' ").

We must be careful to note all that is intended by the term *realistic*. The reader is at first perplexed, for Macedonio seems to heap together all forms of art that are in any way representational, condemning them all with the same epithet. His undiscriminating use of the term leads one to suspect a wider and wider basis of discord. *Realismo* is not merely a particular movement in literature, nor even all art of representational technique: *Realismo* comes to signify for Macedonio the characteristic literary expression of the Western world.

What the Western world has called literature has been the exclusive product of the principle of verisimilitude:

> All realism in art seems to be a result of the fact that there happen to be mirrorlike materials; because of this some shopkeepers thought up the idea of literature, that is, whipping up copies of things. And what is called Art seems to be the product of a peddler of mirrors who has become obsessed, who goes from house to house begging everyone to put all his money in mirrors rather than in things. In every moment of our lives there are scenes, plots, and characters; the product of mirror-art calls itself realistic, but what it does is intercept our view of reality by putting a copy up in front of our eyes. (M, p. 109)

This important passage is not only a repudiation of Western literature, as Noé Jitrik observes, but of its fundamental principle, the principle of verisimilitude:

> the result of copying, then, is "Literature," not reality but "realism":

" . . . and what is called Art seems to be the product of a peddler of mirrors who has become obsessed," etc.

Therefore, what we have is a denial of Literature, that system which we know, but moreover a denial of its fundamental principle, verisimilitude, which cannot help engendering it. ("La 'novela futura,' " p. 42).

Jitrik goes on to point out that the initial repudiation of the copy leads to a series of denials culminating in the repudiation of the literary work:

Literature is a concept which indicates an abstraction, or at least a kind of whole: verisimiltude gives rise to each of the components of this whole, the "works," each of which is a result of the "copy" and of "realism" at its first level of application. A nonrealist aesthetic, therefore, is conceived or divined by Macedonio from the vantage of his denials of the "copy," of "verisimilitude," of the "Work," and of "literature." Of all these terms there is one at which all converge and which permits us to reconstruct the whole circuit: the "Work," the concrete example, the object of the realist aesthetic; as a consequence, the nonrealist aesthetic must seek an object which is not the "Work," something which may be what we have been calling "text" and which Macedonio had no name for since he calls it "novel." (Ibid., p. 43).

The Western concept of the work of art, the finished product of an individual author, perfectly recapitulates our common notion of cosmic creation, our unconscious assumption that "the physical world is an artifact . . . something made or constructed. . . . The idea that (it) is

E

a ceramic creation is a basic image that has entered very deeply into the common sense of most people who have lived in the Western world."[6] Macedonio's repudiation of the work, of the opus absolutely conceived, begun, and finished by an author, is a repudiation of our common "ceramic" conception of creation. Macedonio envisioned as alternative to the work a text whose dynamism exemplified his conception of reality as a continuous flow of "states created out of nothing and incessantly extinguished into nothingness."

The hypothetical "text that is not a work" will be a product not of verisimilitude but of the faculty of *la inventiva*: "Our aesthetic is creativity"; "an author's effectiveness is his capacity to invent." In contrast to the static, definitive product of verisimilitude, the product of *la inventiva* has a tentative, permutable character. But the text-in-the-making, like the work, is inevitably an object existing in time and committed to paper. The ultimate insurance of its dynamism lies in a peculiar articulation of its elements that does not oblige them to occur in a particular sequence or assume a particular pattern—or even to be included—in a given reading of the text. I am referring to what has been called the open structure of the text, a theme developed with revealing insight by Alicia Borinsky de Risler in her valuable study of *Museo* ("Humorística, novelística, y obra abierta en Macedonio Fernández"). *Museo* "ends," for example, with the following note from the author:

To Whoever Would Like to Write This Novel

(Final Prologue)

I leave an open book: perhaps it will be the first "open book" in literary history, that is, the author, wishing that it were better, or at least good, and convinced that its mutilated structure is a dreadful discourtesy to the reader, but also convinced that the book is rich in suggestions, hereby authorizes any future writer whose temperament and circumstances favor intense labor to correct it and to freely edit it, with or without mentioning my name. The task will not be small. Delete, amend, change, but, if possible, let something remain. (M, p. 236)

But *Museo* is not only open at the end but on all sides. Who can be sure, for example, when the "novel" begins? On page 119, where Macedonio indicates that it begins? In the first of the fifty-six prologues? At some indeterminate point partway through the prologues, the point at which the reader at last forms a concept of the "novel" that is ostensibly within the book? And within the "novel"—wherever it lies—the integration of the various elements it contains is a matter of individual preference. The reader is encouraged not to read the book straight through but to skip ahead, go back, omit passages, and, when necessary, throw the book on the floor in irritation! His book may lack a plan, Macedonio insists, but at least it does not pretend to a deceitful congruence.

The disorder of my book is that of all apparently well-ordered lives and works.
Congruence, the execution of a plan, whether in a novel, a work in psychology or biology, or a metaphysics, is a false illusion; this holds for the literary world and probably for the artistic and scientific worlds as well.
For continuity, congruence, and executed plans to exist outside of textbooks and treatises is as fantastic

as for continuity to exist in the reader or student of these books. (M, p. 93)

The technique of nonrealism, then, consists in causing the structure of the work to remain open, keeping the elements in a state of perpetual ionization. The author must work actively to defeat the process of "crystallization." Drastic measures are required to prevent the synthesis of the elements into a stable composition:

> It is in Art that I make my challenge to Verisimilitude, to that deformed intruder in Art, Authenticity. My challenge renders ridiculous anyone which embraces a Dream demanding all the while that it be Real. It culminates in the use of incongruities, to the point of forgetting all about the identity of the characters and their continuity along with such things as temporal sequence, causes before effects, etc., for which reason I invite the reader not to stop to try to untangle absurdities or rationalize contradictions but to allow himself to be carried along by the emotional impetus which the reading of this novel gradually arouses in him. (M, p. 38).

The work of verisimilitude is inevitably bound by the principles of congruence, coherence, "causes before effects," and the like, because the need to achieve a certain purpose or objective commits it to a fairly rigid ordering of its materials. Even the fantastic tale, as is often pointed out, while it may tamper with one of these principles, must adhere rigorously to all the others in order to achieve its preconceived effect upon the reader. But as Jitrik observes, since Macedonio has proposed "an objective-less novel," the ordering of the elements within the text is completely flexible.

. . . therefore, the figure which these [elements] organize or propose is, rather than that of a model of a "novel" or a "text" which might inaugurate a new normative system, that of an idea, a hypothesis about what a novel might be were it not held hopelessly in thrall by the paralyzing exigencies of Verisimilitude. ("La 'futura novela,' " pp. 58–59)

The elements of Macedonio's text are permutable. The prologues can change place, the scenes of the novel as well, Jitrik concludes, without essential change to the text; it is precisely the consistency of order itself, *la pretensión de congruencia,* which is being contested.

To sum up thus far, the *tentative estética* of *Museo* is a calculated attempt to vaporize all the axes along which a work of literature might crystallize. Chronology is confounded, causality is rendered inoperative, narrative development yields to digression. Interruptions, abrupt halts, retrogressions, circular arguments, repetitions, and a thousand impertinencies abort what we usually think of as "narration"; the author/work/reader circuit is disrupted at every moment; from the edges—"beginning" and "ending" inward—no structure is permitted to close.

The text-in-the-making cannot have a fixed and therefore easily identifiable structure; its essential nature is the opposite of this. "Groping in the void, I am experimenting with a technique for a new novel," Macedonio wrote to Gómez de la Serna. "Groping in the void" is perhaps the exact description for what Macedonio was doing. It is indeed difficult to imagine what the alternative to the literary work might be, for the concept of the work is fundamental to our whole way of thinking about art.

Jitrik observes that it is therefore not surprising that Macedonio's ideal is a rather elusive entity:

> All (or almost all) Western thought requires that there be on one side an author, on another a work and on a third side a reader, each in the proper place, creating a circuit in which the Work is central—a product which can be bought and sold, which is producible and consumable. On the other hand, the "text-in-the-making" contrasts with this image, and therefore, since the image of the Work is so solid, its physiognomy may well be rather imprecise. ("La 'futura novela,'" p. 46)

This is a critical point. The text-in-the-making is not readily discernible, because try as he will, Macedonio cannot isolate it. In the three decades he devoted to the preparation of *Museo*, Macedonio discovered that the theoretical "novel" of Belarte could not be realized without recourse to the traditional elements of fiction, without constant reference to the system of literature it proposed to confound.

Interestingly, Macedonio devised the plan of publishing simultaneously "the last bad novel" and "the first good novel." The original project was to bind both books in one volume: *Adriana Buenos Aires* (*última novela mala*) and *Novela de la Eterna* (*primera novela buena*). Macedonio wrote *Adriana Buenos Aires* for amusement in 1922. It is a pulp novel, a veritable catalogue of fictional clichés: amorous intrigue, cliff-hanging suspense, ludicrous coincidence—in short, everything that the seasoned reader of bad novels could possible wish for.* Macedonio at one

---

* *Adriana Buenos Aires* (*Ultima novela mala*), was released for publication in 1974 as Volume 5 of the projected *Obras completas*

point planned to use this text as visible backdrop for his "novel" by binding the two books in one. He abandoned this plan, however, in favor of a considerably more insidious one. In the first prologue of *Museo*, "What Is Born and What Dies," he writes,

Today we present to the public the last bad novel and the first good one. Which one is better? To keep the reader from simply choosing the one of his preferred genre and spurning the other, we have ordained that both books be sold together, an indivisible purchase; although we haven't been able to make it

de Macedonio Fernández, Ediciones Corregidor. Writing the "last bad novel" turned out to be more difficult than writing the "first good novel", Macedonio confesses in *Adriana Buenos Aires:* "Imagine the effort it has cost me to avoid making this novel a work of genius: It is not surprising that when I tried to commission it I encountered so many modest people who said they did not have the requisite lack of talent for the job. And it is certainly harder to write a *bad novel in bad faith* than to write a good one in good faith. And another reminder: don't get them mixed up:"

Despite his best efforts, Macedonio failed to produce not only the *last* bad novel, but even a decent example of the genus. For the author's irrepressible irony defeats his every attempt at *novelón* solemnity, and as a result, the most tear-sodden passages delight rather than depress.

It is not difficult to recognize the recent widower, Macedonio Fernández, in the figure of the protagonist, Don Eduardo de Alto, a forty-five-year-old man who moves into a dubious *pensión*, where he falls in love with the young and appetizing Adriana, Adriana, however, is desperately in love with Adolfo, whose child she is carrying ("He loved me so much that I shall bear his child; it will be a boy and will be named Adolfo," she tearfully confesses to Eduardo). Adolfo, naturally, is insane, and thus unable to perform the honorable act. "What role should the vulnerable Eduardo play in this tragic situation?" we can imagine

obligatory to *read* both books, at least we have the
consolation of having thought up the idea of the
no-money-back purchase of the one one doesn't
want to buy but which is nondetachable from the one
one does want; the Obligatory novel will thus be
either the last bad novel, or the first good one, as the
Reader's taste determines.

It is true that I have sometimes run the risk of
mixing up the bad stuff I had to think up for *Adriana
Buenos Aires* with the good that never stopped coming
to me for *The Novel of Eterna*; the reader will simply
have to lend a hand and sort it all out. Sometimes I
got confused when the wind blew the pages around,
because, as you may have guessed, every day I wrote a
page for each book, and when they got mixed up, I

an announcer asking. Eduardo's emotional dilemma is further
complicated by the arrival of archly beautiful, seventeen-year-
old orphan Estela de Paredes, who, while requiring of Eduardo
some fatherly advice, attempts to seduce him. Failing, she enlists
his aid in launching her career as a "courtesan," a public relations
venture in which Eduardo is aided by a curious cast of characters:
"el andaluz, Dabove, Racq, Borges, Scalabrini, Gómez, Mitchell
y Adriana y Dina. . . . ."

A typical passage of *Adriana Buenos Aires* describes Estella's
capacity for ravishment, the author commenting on his own
literary excesses:

"Estella is a beautiful damsel," I continue. "Black are her
eyes, and they gleam in the night of her full black tresses
like stars of the horizon upon a cloth of moonlight, which is
her forehead. Her nose is small and her nostrils quiver ever
so slightly, which I take to be a sign of a dormant volup-
tuousity. . . . The oval of her face is delicate, and it tells me
that Estella's soul would eschew all things sensual, were it
able, while her lightly pursed lips form a kiss which is perhaps
a look of lingering anger. Her appearance suggests a potential
for happiness and therefore for tragedy. It suggests that

couldn't tell which was which. I had nothing to go by, because the page numbering was the same and so was the quality of the ideas, the paper, and the ink—I had tried hard to be equally intelligent in both books so

Estella cannot know happiness without companionship.[1] Any man to know the kiss of her beautiful mouth would fall passionately in love with her, would never be able to leave her side and would blindly go on pursuing her until she either loved him in return or both of their lives were erased from the world. This is her tragedy: if she kisses, be forewarned that she will never kiss another. If she chooses the wrong man as the love of her life, she will be stricken, she will cease to be. . . . Her first kiss will be her nuptials and will bring her either happiness or death. Estella is tall, which means, I believe, that she will not allow herself to be loved more than she loves in return.[2] (*Obras completas,* 5:213–14).

[1] Let the forced perfection of the model phrases of the bad novel be appreciated: without them I could not keep my promise of presenting the best and last novel of the genre of the bad. Let the reader enlarge upon the psychological profundities and subtleties which they suggest; the lachrymose and grandiloquent phrase and the self-assured psychological probing are a supreme fulfillment of the desideratum of the genre. These difficulties make the *bad novel* harder to write, in my opinion, than the good one. As you see, it is only solemn literature which is easy—a joy to write—for any writer. Anyone . . . can write, with complete ease, an Ode to the Torrid Zone or to the Ruins of Italica, but a demanding bad novel will not tolerate fools. *Odio l'ussata poesia. | Concede commoda al volgo | y fioschi fianchi.* Carducci.

[2] This is shameful; in 1922 I thought I was writing a great novel. It is painful to emerge from this innocent conviction."

In addition to its whimsical story line, *Adriana Buenos Aires* contains numerous digressions, personal and profound asides on love, death, and, of course, metaphysics. A failure on two counts as the "last bad novel," *Adriana Buenos Aires* contains some of Macedonio's most engaging pages.

that my twins would not be jealous of each other.
How I suffered when I couldn't tell whether a brilliant page belonged to the last bad novel or to the
first good one! (M, p. 15)

Both novels are in the book—somewhere. It falls to
the reader to discern the "good" novel and spurn the
"bad." In keeping with its Idealist origins, the novel of
Belarte is not conceived as a "solid object" of knowledge;
the activity of the reader is as critical to its realization as
that of the author. Heightening the reader's consciousness
of the importance of his participation, Macedonio suggests to him that his performance as a reader is being
judged:

I have the good fortune to be the first writer able
to address the double reader, and abusing my advantage, I stoop to beg each of my readers to write
and tell me which of the two novels turned out to be
the obligatory one for him. If you wish to form an
opinion of the work, I would like to form an opinion
of the reader. (M, p. 16)

This could be taken for a tactical ploy, a means of
putting down the opposition by implying that those who
concluded that the emperor was merely naked were just
not sufficiently perceptive. But Macedonio is not dodging
responsibility for his creation but stating metaphorically
the paradoxical interdependence of the "good" and "bad"
novels. Nonrealism cannot be conceived without reference
to realism, and the "text-in-the-making" is necessarily
fashioned of the literary elements that our culture provides. The "novel," like the novel, is made of characters,
scenes, episodes, and the like—the usual elements of

fiction. While Macedonio will distort these elements until they are scarcely recognizable, he cannot dispense with them entirely. As Jitrik points out, the presence of these elements makes it possible for us to perceive the "good" novel.

Jitrik goes on to make a fundamental assertion: the "badness" of the bad novel derives *not from the elements themselves but from a certain conception of them:*

> There is obviously a leap which means that despite the denials there is an affirmation, that of the "elements," whose variations, although barely glimpsed, at least make it possible to see what a "good" novel might be like. On the other hand, what constitutes the "badness" of a bad novel can be clearly understood: it is a certain conception of these elements which causes them to be formalized or crystallized as they are executed. I believe that this is a fundamental point in Macedonio's system and that it has on this account important critical significance. It is as if the old novel, which is the Novel as we know it, had somehow covered up a truth hidden in its own origins which we must now get back to and retrieve. ("La 'futura novela,' " p. 38)

What is the "misconception of the elements" that causes them in the bad novel to "crystallize"? As early as 1929 Macedonio was concerned with the problem. He wrote to Francisco Luis Bernárdez,

> Once we eliminate essay writing (dogmatic, doctrinaire, absolutely spurious art of sociologists and metaphysicians), it remains to be discovered whether or not realism and all imitative art may not be equally doctrinaire and spurious, since it informs us about

reality just as science does: it is as bad as a fictionalized
chemistry would be. But a realism which made use of
materials not as assertions but as signs, as a technique
for evoking "states" [of awareness] . . . could such a
realism be justified? ("Fragmento sobre la metáfora,"
p. 83)

Here Macedonio identifies two possible uses of materials:
they may be used "as assertions, as materials," or they may
be used "as signs, as a technique for evoking states of
awareness." Macedonio's conception of the "novel" of
the future centers around this second, conceptual use of
the elements of fiction. The referential, informative use of
these elements, Macedonio will conclude in later notes on
the novel, leads ultimately to the kind of crystallization
Jitrik mentions. Western fiction, since it is by and large
the product of the use of the elements of experience "as
assertions, as materials," has consistently failed to produce
"novels," according to Macedonio. All we have read thus
far, he insists, are "quasi novels" or "protonovels."

Here, dear public of avid novel readers, I have to
disillusion you: in the course of many centuries you
believe that you have read an infinite number of
novels, that you have enjoyed yourselves to the
utmost, absorbing a thousand plots, episodes, and
pages; but you have not read a single novel, because
those lines of print did not give you what I shall call:
created reading [lectura hecha], but mere allusions,
without technique, to themes which pleased you,
the mere mention of which was sufficient to unlock
your imagination; what you have really been enjoying is your own treasure trove of emotional
fantasy. ("Doctrina estética de la novela," p. 415)

What has delayed the arrival of the "novel" has been the arrest of the literary process at the referential level, the absorption of author and reader in the process of naming and recognizing: dazzled by their mutual "*tesoros de fantasía emocional*," they have attended to the intrinsic interest of the materials themselves rather than to their conceptual or evocative potential.

We can begin to understand the rationale of Macedonio's disruptive literary praxis; it is an effort to prevent the fixation of the fictional process at the referential level, to prevent the crystallization of the materials into a "work." Macedonio will do whatever is necessary to prevent the closing of the text along any axis—logical, chronological, or psychological. By continually lobbing stones into the pool of Aristotelian verisimilitude, he will keep its waters in constant motion, prevent their ever settling into a reflecting surface. Illusion is thus the defeat of art; the author must work actively to keep the reader from "hallucinating": "I want the reader to be constantly aware that he is reading a novel and not witnessing living—not watching 'life.' The moment the reader falls into Hallucination, the ignominy of Art, I have lost, not gained a reader" (M, p. 39).

The "lucidity" of the reader, his perfect consciousness of himself as *reader,* is indispensable insurance against the "closing" of the text. The hermetic novel-worlds praised by Ortega must be left behind, relics of the age of the protonovel. The author himself must contrive to work in the same state of lucidity, according to Macedonio. Dispersing the mists of romantic inspiration, the writer must exercise the most rigorous, deliberate control over the creative process. Recording the images of some "poetic delirium" does not qualify as art:

Even the genre of fantastic literature is realism, in
my opinion, because it is a copying of the inner world,
the world of the imagination; copying is copying,
whether of external perceptions or of internal images.
To copy, to narrate fantasies, even dreams and nightmares, is not art: there are a million nightmares in
every human head and were they all exposed in print,
they would not have the slightest interest. ("Sobre
'Belarte,' " p. 43)

It follows that the credibility of a work of art must
be established on a new basis. The "novel" is not to be
credible as a plausible or authentic representation of real
or possible happenings. On the contrary, "Art only begins
on the other side of Verisimilitude" (M, p. 109). What
matters is not the truth of life, but "the truth of Art,
intrinsic, unconditional, and self-authenticating." The
novel is a narrative "which holds our interest without our
believing in it, and which serves to keep the reader distracted so that, from time to time, literary technique may
operate upon him" ("Doctrina estética," p. 417).

The essence of art is technique: "todo el arte está en la
técnica o versión." It follows logically enough that art fails
when its appeal is primarily to the intrinsic interest of its
materials. "The instrument or medium of art ought not
to be itself intrinsically pleasurable, a condition which is
not met by colors in painting or by voluptuous chords in
music" ("Sobre 'Belarte,' " p. 43).

The most "insipid"—and therefore most "noble"—
instrument of art is the written word, "that uniform and
insipid scrawl which, because it is such, contains not the
slightest taint of sensory appeal, which is impurity in art"
("Sobre 'Belarte,' " p. 42). Of all the arts, only literature
has at its disposal a perfectly *insipid* medium. No other art

has such enormous potential; the written word is the only medium capable of producing an art worthy of the level of consciousness of modern man:

> Belarte Conciencial, the only kind of art worthy of the spiritual enlightenment of contemporary man as well as of his present level of mental acumen . . . has found its organ of expression—completely pure because of its intrinsic insipidness: writing. I see no hope that any other medium might ever lead to any other Belarte; I cannot imagine any other organ that would be absolutely nonsensuous, insipid. (PR44, p. 185)

Of all the diverse media of art, the written word, then, is the "purest," the most nearly "nonsensuous" (*asensorial*). This makes the written word the perfect instrument of Macedonio's Idealist aesthetic, an instrument nearly independent of the sensible world. Through the medium of the written word, the self-authenticating, conceptual art Macedonio aspired to becomes a theoretical possibility. Humanity, however, has thus far not discovered this "noble" function of the word:

> Humanity, which for centuries has possessed this sign—divine in its total lack of sensory appeal— has never discovered the genuine, artistic use of the Word. On the contrary, with slavish dedication it has been satisfied to go on despoiling it of its divine potential through its predilection for sonorities and its ridiculous penchant for rhyming and metering, its childish search for the most shopworn associations between "words" and "a sense of life." The tendency has been to taint the word with life and to extol the copy with absolute servility. (PR44, p. 186)

What is the "genuine, artistic use of the Word" which has been neglected for so many centuries? Macedonio does not specify it, but his own use of language provides some clues. Insisting that words must be "perfectly insipid," he deems "inartistic" any use of them that exploits their sensible properties. In prose and poetry alike, for example, he spurns all auditory recourses. His poetry is devoid of rhyme, assonance, onomatopoeia, and alliteration. His verses are ametrical, often relaxing into what appear to be long paragraphs of prose. His humor never depends on phonic plays on words, or puns, nor is there in his prose any of the Joycean type of visual wordplay. The apparently deliberate cacophonies he occasionally produces call attention to the linguistic norms of Belarte, which vigorously reject musicality in literature. It is not musicality per se that is condemned, of course, but the system of values that in any context exalts the sensible over the conceptual.

It is the conceptual potential of language that interests Macedonio. He rarely uses a word in a way that calls attention to its condition as an "artifact," an object of the senses existing in time and space within a given social milieu. There are no etymological analyses in his metaphysics, for example, nor does he elsewhere play upon the root meanings of words for rhetorical effect. He avoids words whose regional, historical, or sociological connotations are overly specific; there is no use of popular speech, jargon, slang, or dialect in any of his work. The most notable peculiarities of his style—his notoriously tortured syntax and his creation of outrageous substantives—both arise from the frustrations encountered in attempting to express his Idealism in a language fashioned for a different world view.

The conventional rhetorical devices of European

languages are avoided by Macedonio because he sees them, in all probability, as excrescences of a detestable *Realismo*. Belarte, the product of his Idealist aesthetic, exploits neither the intrinsic sensible properties of words—their sound, texture, bulk, rhythm, visual aspect, and the like— nor their sociological or historical connotation. Belarte depends almost exclusively for its effect upon the exploitation of one aspect of language: its conceptual possibilities. This exclusive use of language signifies nothing less than the relegation of the sensible world—the world of history—to a category of minimal importance, and the exaltation of the timeless activity of the mind. The language of Belarte is fundamental evidence of its Idealist origins.

The "artistic" use of the elements of fiction parallels the "artistic" use of the word. Interest is deliberately shifted away from the elements themselves and toward their conceptual possibilities. The intrinsic interest of theme, setting, plot, and the like, must be deemphasized in Belarte. Literature that makes its appeal to the inherent qualities of its ingredients is not art, but "culinary science": "Because art is emotion, a state of the spirit, and never sensation. Therefore I term 'culinary' any kind of art which exploits the sensual for its intrinsic appeal and not for its potential for evoking emotion" ("Sobre 'Belarte,' " p. 43).

In contrast to the "culinary" use of the elements of fiction, Belarte centers interest upon "execution," the manner in which the materials are manipulated by the author. The materials themselves are of merely incidental importance:

The "subject" [*asunto*] is completely lacking in artistic value; . . . execution is the only value in art.

To classify topics as better or worse, or as more or less
interesting, is to talk about ethics: to do the aesthetic is
to artistically execute any topic whatsoever. Any-
body can find a topic; they are superabundant: the
pages of art are extremely scarce; they are produced
with the desperation, the tears and the wrath of Labor.
(M, p. 107)

The purpose of the materials of fiction is to serve as
a kind of springboard, a pretext for the operation of
technique: "Topics are extraartistic. They have no
artistic worth. They are mere pretexts for the exercise
of technique. The horror of art is narrative [*el relato*] and
description" ("Doctrina estética de la novela," p. 413).
Since the function of the elements of fiction differs
greatly from their function in the traditional novel, it is
natural that their form should be radically altered in the
novel of Belarte. Each element must enhance the dynamic,
open character of the text. Macedonio's transformation of
the traditional literary character may serve as an example.

The familiar rounded character of fiction is reduced by
Macedonio to near transparency. Attention is deliberately
directed away from the physical presence of the character.
This process, incidentally, provides some of the book's best
humor. The characters in *Museo* have *no* physiology, for
example, eliminating once and for all the nuisance of
providing for their endless biological functions, their
tiresome infirmities and indispositions.

Besides, I am certain that no live person has gotten
into the narrative, for characters with physiology,
besides being handicapped by sickness and fatigue,
belong to the realist aesthetic, and our aesthetic is not
realist, but creative. (M, p. 20)

According to the author, characters, rather than being seen whole, should be only partially discerned, in "rather misty glimpses . . . of scenes and episodes which are rapidly cut away" (M, p. 40). These transparent, truncated figures, reduced to a strange name—"Quizagenio" ("Perhaps-a-Genius"), "Dulce Persona" ("Dearperson")— and one or two peculiar attributes, recall nothing so much as the figures in Cubist painting. The very evanescence of these figures imbues them with a strange vitality and affords them a curious persistence in the mind, exactly as Macedonio suggests: "The theory is that the characters and events which are skillfully truncated are those which stick in the memory" (M, p. 112).

Cubists believed that introducing the illusion of the third dimension denaturalized the image, depriving it of its essential nature as a painted object; similarly, Macedonio was convinced that the literary character ought not to be made to *seem* real: the character that comes to life is deprived of his essential nature as object of art. Seeming alive is the opposite both of being alive and being fictional; the literary character, to be "real," that is, literary, must be rigorously *fictional*.

What I do not want and have intervened twenty times to prevent in my pages is for the characters to seem alive, and this occurs every time the reader has a hallucination of the reality of an episode: the truth of life, the copy of life, is my abomination. Is not the genuine failure of art, its greatest and perhaps only frustration, its abortion, simply the point at which a character seems to come to life? I allow characters to covet life, to want to live, to attempt to live—but not to seem alive in the sense that their behavior appears real; I abhor all realism. (M, p. 41)

The creations that have been revered as literary characters *par excellence* do not even qualify as literary personages:

Realistic art which is not Belarte, the art of Anna
Karenina, Madame Bovary, Don Quixote, Mignon,
lacks characters; that is, the former do not dream of
being, because they believe they are copies.

To be a character is to dream of being real. And
what is magical in characters, what is seductive and
charming in them, the element which forms their
being and which they alone possess, is not the author's
dream of them, what he makes them think and do,
but their own dream of being, the dream into which
they plunge so eagerly. (M, p. 41)

It is obvious that Macedonio is interested not in the
characters themselves, but, as is the case with the other
elements of fiction, in the conceptual possibilities they
afford. Above all, he is interested in fiction's potential for
the play of ontological planes; the fictional character is,
according to Macedonio, "a prodigious instrument of
ontological disruption." The deliberate confusion of the
various modes of existence of character, reader, and author
can afford a fictional narrative a remarkable transcendence:
"This deliberate confusionism probably has a high
potential for ontological liberation" (M, p. 37).

As we have noted, fiction and metaphysics for Macedonio were two versions of the same activity. Fiction was
"nondiscursive metaphysics." Metaphysics as defined in
No toda es vigilia was the activity which by any path led to
the moment of "pure vision." Macedonio believed that
such moments of enlightenment could occur in the

reading of a fictional narration. In a number of passages he attempts to describe the nature of this *satori*-like effect, but despite his efforts the concept remains obscure. He incorporates the achievement of this effect into his earliest definitions of the novel: In "The Aesthetic Doctrine of the Novel" he refers to the effect as a kind of vertigo (*mareo*) of the sense of self:

> In short, a novel is a narrative which holds our interest without our believing in it, and which serves to keep the reader distracted so that, from time to time, literary technique may operate upon him, producing in him an ontological vertigo [*el mareo de su certidumbre de ser*], a vertigo of the self ("Doctrina estɪtica de la novela," p. 417).

In later texts he refers to the effect as "the disruption of the certainty of being." His essay "Toward a Theory of Humor" begins with a reference to this effect. Here again, the effect is held to be the definitive element of Belarte.

> In my long pursuit of pure art, of a perfect non-realism, I have settled upon a final definition: Belarte is solely that work of the intelligence which does not propose to deal with a particular topic or facet of consciousness but to produce a disruption of the certainty of being, of existing within a whole, and which does not rely upon ratiocination in order to achieve that end. (PR44, p. 185)

There are several references to the effect in the lessons on aesthetic theory provided for the characters and readers in the prologues to *Museo*. At one point Macedonio observes that the reason literature does not exist is that writers have not devoted themselves exclusively to producing moments of *"la conmoción de la certeza de ser."*

Literature does not exist because of its failure to devote itself exclusively to producing this effect of disidentification, the only end which might justify its existence and which only this Belarte is capable of producing. (M, p. 35)

Macedonio believes that he himself has achieved the effect only a few times:

If in each one of my books I have succeeded in producing two or three times this effect which I shall call in familiar language a suffocation, an extinction of the certainty of personal continuity, during which the reader slides away from himself, this is all I hope to accomplish as regards means; with respect to ends, I sought liberation from the notion of death: the evanescence, mutability, rotation, alterability of the self is what makes it immortal, that is to say, not linked to the destiny of a body. (M, p. 35)

The desired effect, then, is nothing less than an intuition of immortality, experienced fleetingly by the reader absorbed in reading a fictional narrative. Macedonio's originality is his affirmation—a paradoxical one in Western tradition—that the self is immortal precisely by virtue of its evanescence.

Common to all the texts we have examined is a reference to a sudden, momentary dissolution of self-awareness: "the disruption of the certainty of being"; "effect of disidentification"; "ontological vertigo"; "vertigo of the

self"; "the extinguishing of the sense of personal continuity." "The loss of the self is a gain," Macedonio had
written in *No toda es vigilia*. The self is not a "diamond,"
Macedonio believed with James (James is invoked,
incidentally, in nearly every passage in which Macedonio
alludes to *la conmoción conciencial*). The self is not a separate,
finite entity residing in a body. This notion of the self
must be repudiated, our uncritical belief in it shaken,
Macedonio insists; belief in a diamantine self engenders,
inevitably, images of its annihilation.

> I only make these affirmations in order to encourage
> the young reader to keep himself always on the
> defensive against the shipwreck-conviction—belief in
> a self whose destiny is linked to the life and death of a
> body. (M, p. 37)

> . . . the certainty of being which gives rise to the
> universal intimidation of the equally absurd and
> vacuous notion of nonbeing. (M, p. 237)

No amount of discursive reasoning can counteract the
"shipwreck-conviction," the fear of nonbeing; logic,
though it is the guardian of life, teaches us that we are
mortal: ". . . this logic . . . says to us each day: 'since
everyone dies, you are going to die,' or, 'there is no effect
without a cause' " (PR44, p. 251).

Such logic must be confounded, and the humorist and
the writer of fiction, or "nondiscursive metaphysics,"
may occasionally succeed where the philosopher fails. A
Zen master may answer the earnest question of a disciple
with an absurd non sequitur, pinch the young man's nose
or strike him with a cane to abruptly cut off the process of
reasoning; such tactics occasionally produce the moment

of enlightenment the disciple has been striving to attain for years. Macedonio seems to believe that the humorist and the novelist may similarly produce the desired result in an individual by employing unorthodox tactics. He identifies two possibilities:

> I believe that without doctrines, explanations, and especially without ratiocinations, two unique and genuinely artistic moments can be created in the mind of the reader: the intuition of "nothing" as an intellectual concept which is possible in conceptual humor, and the intuition of an ontological "nothing" which is possible when the characters in a novel are properly used, that is, when they are used not to make us believe in what is being narrated but in order to make the reader believe, for a brief moment, that he is a character, that he has been snatched from life.

> I think it is a virtue when an aesthetic technique can disturb, disrupt our sense of ontological security along with our great "principles of reason," our intellectual security. (PR44, p. 186, 250–51)

Numerous contemporary writers of fiction have capitalized on the vertiginous concepts of Idealism. Magic realists, for example, have relied heavily on the postulations and paradoxes of Berkeley, Bradley, Schopenhauer—and Macedonio Fernández. But these writers have consistently created their stories within conventional literary forms and in accordance with the principles of verisimilitude. A story like "The Circular Ruins," for example, although it postulates an Idealist world, is in itself a perfect example of the classic tale as defined by Poe:[7] a story whose ending or last sentence determines everything preceding it. Macedonio is unique in attempting to write fiction in accordance with a rigorously Idealist *theory* of literature.

In attempting this, he set for himself an extraordinarily difficult task, for no models exist for such creation. The lack of precedent may account in part for the heavy theoretical content of *Museo*. Belarte had to create and expound its own norms in terms that would be intelligible to a reader habituated by all his experience to the literature of verisimilitude. For Macedonio deliberately to confound the principles of identity, congruence, and rational development was to invite suspicions of mental derangement. Anderson Imbert's summary dismissal of Macedonio as "loco" ("he wrote little because literature did not interest him")[8] gives evidence of the danger in challenging the validity of accepted cultural norms.

Why struggle against insuperable difficulties, "grope in the void" to bring forth an unprecedented form of fiction? We can only speculate about the motives behind the creation of Belarte Conciencial, but one thing seems clear: for Macedonio, the usual aesthetic product of our culture, the work of art, could not but suggest finitude; Macedonio's aim, it would seem, was to create a sign of eternality. To this end, perhaps, he struggled to realize the hypothetical text-in-the-making, the "novel" that might signify through its dynamism the eternal and totally free activity of the mind.

Chapter IV

Character and Self-Image in Belarte

A good portrait does not express a character but simply a single moment of one from which nothing can be inferred about the character as a whole, because the *congruence* of individual character is a senseless concept: from no trait is it possible to infer any other (and the same could be said about the Cosmos, about all Reality), and no character trait contradicts any other trait. ("Inéditos de Macedonio," *Hispamérica* 1 (1972): 52

"The world is not given"; the world view that posits a cosmic donor giving the world to a recipient self was erroneous, Macedonio believed. Equally erroneous was the literary circuit that reiterates this view, that of an author giving his completed work to a reader. Macedonio's herculean project throws into crisis each of the elements in this familiar circuit: in Belarte, "author" is a problematical concept, "work" is not a coherent object of

137

knowledge, and "reader" is anything but the passive recipient of the author's "work." But this is not all; the very articulation of the circuit is systematically interrupted. Macedonio does not *give* a novel to the reader. The novel the reader expects recedes from his grasp as reliably as the grapes of Tantalus. All his experience as reader has conditioned him to expect a novel (perhaps it begins on the next page, surely it is somewhere in the book), and Macedonio fully exploits this expectation, manipulating to his advantage the reader's anxiousness to discover the "answer" to the riddle of *Eterna*.

A Zen disciple struggles earnestly to solve the *koan* given by his master, for all his experience has taught him that his intellect is equal to the task of discovering the hidden congruence behind the enigmatic words. When riddle solving has been transcended and *satori* is achieved, no one imagines that the master has *given* enlightenment to the disciple; but the master's stratagems and incitements were indispensable to its attainment. Macedonio's novelistic praxis is of the same order; he does not, therefore, narrate in the usual etymological sense. The ancient image of the *gnarus,* the one who knows, spinning a yarn that informs his hearers of the world, still dominates our thinking about fiction. Macedonio saw a different function for the narrator; his concern would be not so much to impart knowledge as to awaken insight. Accordingly, the text itself would have a different nature, for the narrator's attention would be fixed beyond his narrative upon the consciousness of the reader:

> Author: You are what concerns me here, reader; you
> in your precarious presence, are my subject.
> Everything else is simply a pretext to hold
> you where my technique can reach you.
> Reader: Thank you. (M, p. 223)

The text, then, is a pretext, or pre-text; what happens in this Idealist literary encounter happens not on the printed page but in the intuition of the reader. The text, therefore, is not "straight"; its incitements and stratagems are not an end in themselves, but a kind of springboard, a means of gaining entry to the reader's consciousness for the purpose of exercising a kind of mental judo, unbalancing questionable assumptions, stimulating an unpredictable response. The concept of text as pre-text ought to be a cardinal point of reference in any critical approach to Macedonio; the specter of the critic arrested at the level of classical textual exegesis of *Museo* is alarming. We ought to be willing in judging Macedonio to run the risk of reenacting the aesthetic process as he conceived it, that is, to rely without apology upon our intuitive response to his incitements.

For the text of *Museo,* as we suggested in the previous chapter, does not constitute a novel, as we have traditionally understood the term. As Noé Jitrik observes, the text is "pure dynamism"; it never "crystallizes." Traces of a novel are tantalizingly "there," but the function of this novel is to be looked for and not found. No amount of forewarning will convince a reader educated in this culture that the book, correctly read, does not contain a novel, so strong are our assumptions that behind names lie coherent wholes, that behind appearances lie congruent patterns of meaning. Leo Bersani reminds us in his seminal study *Balzac to Beckett* that

we live in a culture where it has been assumed for two thousand years that the world is the *sign* of the truth. Significance precedes experience, which is both expressive and deceptive and which therefore needs to be decoded or interpreted. No one has ever

perceived an identity; it is behind phenomena, and the
latter are self-effacing signs which point to their
invisible source. Experience is a mystery story in a
world where the truth is always a hidden referent.
The prototype of Western civilization is Oedipus
Rex: all things are puzzling enigmas, but behind the
enigmas lie perfectly designed plans of human destinies. (p. 4)

It is inevitable that we look for the hidden novel, the
secret meaning behind the lines of text of *Museo;* every
habit of mind our culture provides inclines us to do
exactly this, as Macedonio is well aware. We are secretly
convinced of the underlying coherence and unity that,
after all, *must* be there. But the function of the *Novela de la
Eterna* is to be not there, to elude our grasp, to perplex and
outmaneuver us in a puzzling display of nonexistence.
What is "liberating" about the frustrating experience of
looking for the *Novela de la Eterna* and not finding it?
What is liberating, Macedonio might counter, about the
experience of looking for the novel in *Germinal* or *Doña
Perfecta* and *finding* it, finding a world of physical dimension operating according to a rigidly conceived causality,
inhabited by characters whose "perfectly designed . . .
destinies" make freedom an illusion?
     Even the most dynamic of the "quasi novels," those
that, we might assume, approached Unamuno's viviparous
ideal, rested upon a view of the self Macedonio believed
humanity was ready to transcend.

The arts of the novel and of [humor] ought to
attune themselves to the agility and capacity for
reflection of the very lucid contemporary mentality.
Let us keep in mind that we are in the century of the

Third Reflection of the Self (the Self thinking about a Self that thought yesterday about the Self). (PR44, p. 251)

Belief in a real self transcendent to experience, a coherent unity behind appearances, was analogous to the erroneous belief in a real world, according to Macedonio. The effect of disidentification he speaks of is that of shaking this belief, exorcising the phantom of a self supposedly more real than its manifestation in consciousness. There is no such transcendent self, Macedonio writes in *No toda es vigilia:* moment to moment, we are our mental experiences and nothing more. Macedonio's literary goal is a psychological or spiritual one as well. To shake the reader's belief in a real self as the source from which his present and future behaviour necessarily derives is to afford him a new dimension of freedom. Macedonio's ideal is to escape, to the extent that language and the workings of the mind permit, both a literature and a psychology of source. His rejection of the copy in art is analogous to his rejection of a derivative view of personality.

In the novel the effect of *desidentificación* is achieved through the agency of the characters as they are used by the author to subvert the reader's habitual response to patterns of identity. In order to understand what Macedonio hopes to accomplish and why he goes about it as he does, let us consider briefly the nature of literary selves in the art of verisimilitude.

Realistic fiction rests upon "secure dualities," Leo Bersani notes. "There is reality and there is the copy or interpretation, and there is the observer and the world he is observing" (*Balzac to Beckett,* p. 8). These dualities ordinarily retain a comforting discreteness: subject and

object retain an always intelligible relationship; behind the
world of appearance lies the stable world of essence. The
novelist reports on the world of his characters in images the
reader recognizes as reflective of an anterior reality; the
reader can theoretically retrace the author's steps, passing
from the copies back to the original, "real" models.
Underlying the whole process is the tacit assumption that
there is an absolute separation between fiction and reality,
and that fiction can ultimately be tested against this reality
more authoritative than itself.

Traditionally, our recognition and understanding of the
fictional world of the novel has depended upon our
identification with the fictional selves who inhabit it. As
Jitrik suggests, the character is the element upon which
rests the system of identifications that gives the realist
system its form.* He goes on to observe,

> And it is understandable that such responsibility
> should have fallen upon the character; in the narrative
> as we know it, it is the character which enables us to
> comprehend what is being narrated; the character is
> the most important structuring element as well,
> inasmuch as the story is told by one human being to
> another, which actualizes the entropomorphic re-
> lationship which governs all human actions. ("Des-
> trucción de formas en las narraciones," p. 224)

In the literature of verisimilitude the surface of a literary
character, his name, details of his physiognomy and
clothing, his profession, tastes, and the like, posit a
conceptual unity ready and waiting to be intuited by the

* ". . . son los personajes el elemento sobre el que reposa el
sistema de identificaciones que da forma al sistema realista. . . ."

reader. We have only to read a few sentences of Taine's *History of English Literature* to be reminded of the force of this assumption and of the implications it has held for the process of characterization:

> On observing the visible man with your own eyes what do you try to find in him? The invisible man. These words which your ears catch, those gestures, those airs of the head, his attire and sensible operations of all kinds are for you, merely so many expressions; these express something, a soul. An inward man is hidden beneath the outward man, and the latter simply manifests the former. You have observed the house in which he lives, his furniture, his costume, in order to discover his habits and tastes, the degree of his refinement or rusticity, his extravagance or economy, his follies or his cleverness. You have listened to his conversation and noted the inflections of his voice, the attitudes he has assumed, so as to judge of his spirit, self-abandonment or gayety, his energy or his rigidity. You consider his writings, works of art, financial and political schemes, with a view to measure the reach and limits of his intelligence, his creative power and self-command, then ascertain the usual order, kind and force of his conceptions, in what way he thinks and how he resolves. All these externals are so many avenues converging to one centre, and you follow these only to reach that centre; here is the real man, namely, that group of faculties and sentiments which produces the rest.[1]

This image of the "real man" existing beneath the surface of appearances, the soul or coherent center of

F

personality, is analogous to a belief in a real world, anterior to experience. Both notions, of course, have been violently assaulted by twentieth-century philosophy and art. Noé Jitrik notes that underlying the dissolution of belief in these formerly stable wholes there is a common epistemological crisis:

> ... the "self-questioning" is not only a generative nucleus which disappears in the form which it produces: we discover it in the form as well, and each time it appears it offers us a double perspective, that of a world the knowledge of which has become doubtful, and at the same time, that of an author who transmits the same kind of doubt about his capacity to know. ... ("Destrucción de formas," p. 221)

The history of the novel from Proust to Robbe-Grillet could probably be written in terms of the writer's response to and participation in the disintegration of these wholes. For many writers the dissolution was the result of skepticism, a disbelief in the possibility of knowledge of any reality, including the self. Vivian Mercier in his book *The New Novel from Queneau to Pinget* resumes a general attitude of the New Novelists:

> All are in some degree skeptical about "reality." Does it exist? And if it does exist, how can we attain any certain knowledge of it? ... Nathalie Sarraute coined the phrase "the age of suspicion" to define the attitude of the modern reader toward modern fiction; it also defines the attitude of the New Novelist toward human experience—his raw material. The very phrase "human experience" begs the question, for it implies on one hand, a *subject* in the technical sense—a

human being who experiences—and on the other hand an *object*—something that this being experiences. The New Novelist finds himself unwilling or unable to make this distinction between subject and object. As a writer, he must then discover, consciously or unconsciously, a technique that will force or inveigle his reader into a similar incapacity. Beckett's *The Unnamable* and Robbe-Grillet's *Jealousy* exemplify two entirely different narrative techniques that achieve this end. Joyce achieved it earlier on an enormous scale in *Finnegan's Wake*; all discussions of who the dreamer is seem bound to prove fruitless: the dream dreams itself, subject and object becoming one in the new language coined by Joyce, just as form and content become one. . . . (p. 4)

Macedonio as well will work upon the reader, forcing or inveigling him into an incapacity to distinguish between the familiar and reassuring dualities of verisimilitude. But it is essential to bear in mind that unlike the writers referred to above, Macedonio proceeds not from suspicion but from faith. The image of the cosmos as a dream without a dreamer, far from being a sign of desolation, had for him the luminosity of mystical revelation. The dissolution of self signified plenitude of being; "the loss of the self is a gain," he tells us in *No toda es vigilia*. A surplus, not a deficit, of faith in being informs Macedonio's insistence on the nullity of the *Yo*.

The importance of this fundamental difference between Macedonio and artists like those discussed in Wylie Sypher's penetrating *Loss of Self in Modern Literature and Art* cannot be overemphasized. For most of the artists discussed by Sypher the loss of self has tragic overtones; it is synonymous with annihiliation. Most of them could speak with Robert Lowell of "the horror of the lost self." Jean Grenier's phrase "We now walk in a universe where there is no echo of 'I' " is the nostalgic leitmotif of Sypher's study. "In Beckett's novels," Sypher writes in his concluding chapter (entitled "The Anonymous Self— A Defensive Humanism"), "it is almost a misnomer to talk of character, for the consciousness of the central figure is vestigial, a vague residue of man's anxieties. *The Unnamable* is a commentary by the obliterated figure called 'I' who stands patiently at the threshold of an existence fringing off into silence—the silence Hamlet feared might be troubled by bad dreams" (p. 147). With few changes this might describe any number of twentieth-century protagonists for whom loss of self is, quite simply extinction.

That the loss of self, far from being tragic, is an absolute desideratum is an idea difficult for this culture to receive. We are prone to confuse ideas of transcending the ego with "loss of ego strength."[2] The nineteenth-century image of the imperious romantic self is still very much with us. Freud, who wrote of his intention to "strengthen the Ego, to enlarge its field of observation as a kind of cultural project 'like the reclamation of the Zuyder Zee,' " regarded the disassociation of self-awareness experienced by the mystic as a regression to infantile narcissism. We find it difficult to think of loss of self as anything but the annihilation of individual in collective nonentity or in a momentary rapture of oceanic consciousness. One source of difficulty is the word "loss." "Loss of self," Macedonio's *desidentificación* does not mean witnessing the destruction of ego, but seeing it for what it is, to "see through it," to use Alan Watts's apt phrase. This "loss" is of course a gain; *"la pérdida del yo es un acrecimiento."* To cause the reader to apprehend the fictitious dimension of selfhood could be considered the central motivation of Macedonio's "novel."

His very first definition of the "novel" (1929), we recall, proclaimed it to be "a tale [*relato*] which holds the reader's interest, although he does not believe in it, and which keeps him distracted so that from time to time, literary technique may operate upon him, producing in him an ontological vertigo [*el mareo de su certidumbre de ser*], a vertigo of the self" ("Doctrina estética," p. 417). *Museo de la novela de la Eterna* is responsible in its entirety to this definition; it would be possible to account for the entire work in terms of its attempt to operate upon the consciousness of the reader for the purpose of achieving this effect.

What seems to have been the germ of this idea was the passage in the *Quijote* when Don Quijote complains that Avellaneda has published an inaccurate record of his deeds. "Think of it!" Macedonio observes,

a "character" with a "history." You will feel dizzy, you will believe that Quixote is alive when you hear him complaining that someone is talking about him, about his life. And there is a more profound vertigo as well: since your mind has become conditioned through a thousand pages of reading to believe the fantastic, you will experience a qualm and wonder with a little shiver whether you, who consider yourself so alive, might really be a fiction, a "character." (1929; "Doctrina estética," p. 417)

The effect achieved by Cervantes is highly praised by Macedonio. The *Quijote*, greatest of all the "quasi novels," was a product of "enthusiasm, but not of technique, a work of great natural but not artistic beauty."

In producing this effect, Cervantes, according to Macedonio, inaugurated "technical or conscious prose," prose
which induces a kind of ontological vertigo. This passage
of the *Quijote* has also attracted the interest of Borges. In
"Magias parciales del Quijote" we read,

> Why should it disturb us to see Don Quixote a
> reader of the *Quixote* and Hamlet a spectator of
> *Hamlet*? I think I know the reason: such inventions
> suggest that if the characters in a piece of fiction can
> be readers or spectators, then we, their readers or
> spectators, may be fictitious.[3]

That both Macedonio and Borges should be moved to
comment on this passage is significant. It is precisely at
this point that the paths of the two thinkers meet and
diverge, the fictitiousness of identity being a revelation of
vastly different consequences for the skeptic and for the
mystic.

What Macedonio hopes will happen in the reader's
consciousness is explained in one of the prologues of
Museo. He says that he does not want the reader to begin
to think of the characters as real; he goes on to say,

> What I want is something quite different, to gain
> the reader as a character, to have him believe for a
> moment that he is not alive. This is a feeling he should
> thank me for, one which nobody else has ever tried
> to procure for him. The reader should know that this
> impression, never before produced in anyone by
> means of the written word, this impression, which I
> should like my novel to introduce into the con-
> sciousness of human beings, is a blessing for all
> conscious life, because it obliterates and frees us from

the purely cerebral fear which we call the dread of nonbeing. Anyone who believes even for an instant that he does not exist and then returns to a belief in his own existence will forever understand that the entire content of the verbalization or notion "nonbeing" is simply the belief in nonbeing. Descartes' metaphysics ought to have originated with an "I do not exist" rather than that unfortunate "I exist"; one cannot believe that he does not exist unless he exists. (M, p. 39)

A few paragraphs later he explains that the shock he is preparing for the reader is "the shock of nonexistence," that of discovering oneself not reading but "being read," being a character (M, p. 40).

The "shock" is recognizing as fictitious the sense of self that equates being, metaphorically, with "being read," being, in other words, as being perceived by others, a sense of self derived from social contact. It is this "choque de inexistencia," or "desidentificación" that Macedonio labors to produce through all the curious strategems of Belarte.

The reader's sense of identity is assaulted in many ways. His sense of continuity, temporality, logic, and coherence with regard to himself is shaken at every turn through conceptual humor, through disturbing metaphysical asides, and through the use of "that prodigious instrument of ontological disruption, the character in a novel" (M, p. 24). The very articulation of the text is a calculated assault upon the principle of continuity. An early prologue announces the inauguration in the book of hopscotch literature (la literatura salteada), a strategy devised, supposedly, to trick the discontinuous reader the who prefers to jump around in a book into reading "straight";

the text is so mixed up that the reader who jumps around may find himself reading a continuous narration. The brunt of this Quevedesque joke appears to be the text, but Macedonio produces a kind of conceptual boomerang that deflects the joke to its true target, the reader:

I do not request, jump-around reader,—who will never admit to having read all of anything yet who will end up reading every bit of my novel, with the result that your jumping around to scramble my original numbering of the pages (it is really pointless to number pages anyway for readers like you) will turn out to have been in vain, because, as we shall see in *The Biography of the Reader,* the book in which the reader will at last be read, the jump-around reader eventually came upon this book, which was so full of kinks that he had no choice but to read it straight in order to preserve the discontinuity of his reading because the book jumped around even before he did —that you forgive me for giving you a discontinuous work, which as such is an interruption for you, since you interrupt youself without any help, and since you have already been disturbed by my prologues in which I, the jump-around author, tried so hard to trick you into imagining that you were an orderly reader that you were actually made to doubt the stability of the identity of your jump-around self. (M, p. 28)

Nearly every instance in which Macedonio apparently ridicules his own text for lack of coherence or plan or continuity is, if closely examined, a pretext to assault the *reader's* pretensions of "congruence." He may begin, for example, by talking about his book, remarking that the disorder of the text is that of all lives and works, which merely appear to be orderly; "what passes for congruence, for the execution of a plan in a novel or even in a work of psychology or biology or metaphysics is a false illusion of the literary world and perhaps of the artistic and scientific worlds as well"; he then adds that what passes for congruence of personality is equally illusory:

> It is a mystification on the part of Kant, of Schopenhauer, almost always of Wagner, of Cervantes, of Goethe, to create in their works an impression of congruity, of having been planned.
>
> For continuity, congruence, and executed plans to exist outside of textbooks and treatises is as fantastic as for continuity to exist in the reader or student of these books. (M, p. 93)

Macedonio, in his assault upon the reader's sense of identity, relies above all upon his knowledge of the reader's response to fiction, his knowledge that the reader will struggle against desperate odds to hear a coherent story. Macedonio plays mercilessly upon the reader's yearning to get on with the story. The story is promised and then postponed in every conceivable way. Fifty-six prologues retard the "start" of what the reader thinks will be the novel. The prologues, anticipatory clarifications, preliminary notes, preparatory gestures with their multifarious digressions, asides, and apostrophes, work unbearably upon the reader's cultural conditioning to resolve, to conclude, finally to consume the product that supposedly awaits him. Stern's digressions in *Tristram Shandy* are of a similar nature and possibly of similar intent.* In *Tristram Shandy*, however, the story of Tristram eventually gets told, although this requires nine books, two of which are required to get the protagonist's legs into his breeches. In *Museo*, whether the story is told or not is problematical; much will depend upon where we decide the story is located in the book, a problem that will concern us in the next chapter. As far as the ostensible plot of Eterna's novel is concerned, Macedonio plays his cruelest trick of all upon the expectant reader, whose anxiety to begin has reached fever pitch, when on page 71 he tells the reader, all in one breath, everything that is going to *happen* in the novel. The reader feels cheated, deceived; that was not what he wanted; a plot summary is no substitute for a novel. "If you think there is a possibility that you might like the novel just summarized, then read it" (M, p. 72), Macedonio observes coolly. The gradual, suspenseful revelation of a plot, what Cortázar calls the "unrolling of a Chinese scroll," is incompatible with Macedonio's purpose, which is precisely to break down the reader's mental habit of conceiving of meaning as solution of a problem, resolution of a conflict, elucidation of an enigma. The good reader, the artist-reader, would not look for such finalizations:

The reader who will not read my novel unless he knows in advance how it comes out is my kind of

*This idea is interestingly developed by Philip Stevick in his essay "Theory of Fictional Chapters" in *The Theory of the Novel*. In speaking of the organization of *Tristram Shandy*, Stevick says, "What this internal, associationist, apparently capricious organization effects is precisely that radical reorientation of the gestalt-making mechanism which I have suggested is possible in fiction, in this case by playing the mind of Tristram against the conventions of fiction" (p. 183).

reader; he is an artist, because the kind of reader who
reads in expectation of an outcome is looking for
something which art ought not to give—he is concerned about conditions of life, rather than states of
awareness; the only artist-reader is the one who does
not care about a solution. (M, p. 73)

If art cannot give "final solutions," what can it give?
Something perhaps more valuable, Macedonio seems
to suggest: a distrust of solutions, or rather an ability to
see through them, to see them as the provisional and
precarious constructs that they are.

But the impulse to solve is one of the fundamental
motivations of the Western world. So powerful is the
reader's cultural conditioning toward resolution that he
is quite easily inveigled into participating in the "making"
of the novel, Macedonio's ultimate strategem. The
reader, eager to make order out of what seems to be chaos,
to discover a pattern, to see development, is completely
vulnerable to the incitements of an author who claims
that he is tired, confused, perplexed, that he does not
know where to go with the novel, how to get it off the
ground. Playing the role of a kind of antiauthor, Macedonio shares his doubts and concerns with the sympa-
thetic reader, who before he knows it catches himself in
the act of trying to "help," of making decisions, of
mentally urging movement in one direction or another
in a hopeless attempt to manipulate the fictional beings
by whom *he*, of course, is being manipulated.* It is at

*This idea of Macedonio's is paralleled in a passage of Cortá-
zar's *Rayuela* in which Morelli outlines his theory of the novel:
". . . hacer del lector un cómplice, un camarada de camino.
Simultaneizarlo, puesto que la lectura abolirá el tiempo del

such moments that Macedonio realizes his literary aim: "What I want . . . is to gain the reader as a character, that is, to have him believe for a moment that he is not alive" (M, p. 39).

A critical element in the process of *desidentificación* is the reader's response to the equivocal nature of the characters. Macedonio speaks repeatedly and confidently of the character as a prodigious instrument of "ontological disruption." The process of characterization, then, the means by which the reader comes to know the characters and to respond to them, is of central importance in the execution of the "novel" of Belarte. But what can be the basis of a technique of characterization in an aesthetic system that denies the pattern-making principles that enable us to identify and to recognize? Macedonio's radical rejection of the usual techniques of characterization may be inferred from the following passage concerning resemblance in (painted) portraits:

A good portrait does not express a character but simply a single moment of one from which nothing

lector y lo trasladará al del autor. Así el lector podría llegar a ser copartícipe y copadeciente de la experiencia por la que pasa el novelista, *en el mismo momento y en la misma forma.* Todo ardid estético es inútil para lograrlo: sólo vale la materia en gestación, la inmediatez vivencial (trasmitida por la palabra, es cierto, pero una palabra lo menos estética posible; de ahí la novela 'cómica', los *anticlimax,* la ironía, otras tantas flechas indicadoras que apuntan hacia lo otro . . . . [Esta novela cómica] le da como una fachada, con puertas y ventanas detrás de las cuales se está operando un misterio que el lector cómplice deberá buscar (de ahí la complicidad) y quizá no encontrará (de ahí el compadecimiento). Lo que el autor de esta novela haya logrado para sí mismo, se repetirá (agigantándose, quizá, y eso sería maravilloso) en el lector cómplice" (pp. 453–54).

can be inferred about the character as a whole, because the *congruence* of individual character is a senseless concept: from no trait is it possible to infer any other (and the same could be said about the Cosmos, about all Reality), and no character trait contradicts any other trait. ("Inéditos de Macedonio," *Hispamérica* 1 (1972.: 52)

In Gide's *Les Faux-Monnayeurs* Edouard observes, "Je ne suis jamais que ce que je crois que se suis et cela varie sans cesse, de sorte que souvent, si je n'étais là pour les accointer, mon être du matin ne reconnaîtrait pas celui du soir. Rien ne saurait être plus différent de moi, que moi-même" (first part, ch. 8). In *No toda es vigilia,* Macedonio, in terms not unlike those of the phenomenologists, had denied the self any separate existence from the succession of mental experiences, "*estados,*" which constitute it. His insistence that a good portrait does not express a character, but only one moment of it, is perfectly consistent with this view of personality. His denial of the "congruence" of individual character, his assault upon the principles of continuity and coherence as they apply to notions of the self, are not arbitrary repudiations of the techniques of realism; these principles are challenged by him not because they forge the literature of verisimilitude, but because they forge a sense of self he considered erroneous and damaging.

But if "from no trait is it possible to infer any other," if the process, so admirably described by Taine, by which the invisible man can be inferred from the visible, is seen as spurious, what *can* be the basis of a technique of characterization? Other questions arise as well; can the precarious personages produced by this new technique, whatever it may be, bear the enormous structural weight

that the characters in a narration have traditionally borne?
(Can we conceive of the character as "conducting wire,"
as Tomashevsky suggests, when the principle of continuity
is precisely what is being questioned?) The narrative as we
understand it rests firmly upon the concept of characters
as structuring elements; there has never been a narrative
without characters, or agents—or at least the world has
not considered texts that lacked such agents narratives.
Moreover, the character in its relation to the selves we
are and encounter in life has always been a touchstone of
literary criticism. Can the character born in the rarefied
atmosphere of Belarte withstand the tests to which it will
inevitably be put?

In Belarte there can be no "characterization" as we have
traditionally understood the term. The process by which
the author through a careful presentation of details or
events induces the reader to infer the invisible man from
the visible is an impossibility, for the principles of identity,
continuity, and the like, which make inference possible,
are precisely those that are being contested. The reader,
in fact, must not be permitted to infer a hidden self
behind the surfaces presented. To begin to perceive other
dimensions, to begin to think of the character as real, is to
hallucinate, in Macedonio's parlance. Hallucination, we
recall, is the "abomination of art" (M, p. 41). The special
province of the character of Belarte is to be rigorously
fictional: for him to begin to seem real is the certain sign
of "the abortion of art."

All of the characters are under contract *to dream of
being,* which is their unique propensity, a state of
mind unattainable by the living and the only genuine
matter of Art. To be a character is to dream of being
real.

Is not the genuine failure of art, its greatest and perhaps only frustration, its abortion, simply the point at which a character seems to come to life? I allow characters to covet life, to want to live, to attempt to live—but not to seem alive in the sense that their behavior appears real; I abhor all realism. (M, p. 41)

The character of Belarte, then, must be presented as pure surface. To suggest another dimension is to denaturalize his existence as object of art. He is a vestigial being, divested of physical characteristics and bodily functions:

characters with physiology . . . belong to a realist aesthetic, and our aesthetic is not realist but creative. (M, p. 20)

nothing of a sensory character (pleasures or discomforts of eating, of smoking, of physiological sexuality, etc.) is a proper subject of art. (M, p. 66)

The usual character of Belarte has no age, no civil, marital, social, economic, or religious status. Upon entering the Novel, the Home of Nonexistence, he is advised to leave his past at the gate. He has no ties to the outside world and is intended as a pure fiction existing solely in and of the novel. To the giant agglomerations of Western fiction from Celestina to Mr. Sammler, Macedonio opposes a kind of personage whose "content" is minimal, a nearly transparent figure, who may epitomize a single concept. Deunamor, for example, has a single attribute: he does not exist. He lost his existence at the time of his bereavement, and his function in the novel is to serve as a foil for the other characters, to allow their existence, through contrast to his nonexistence, to appear more substantial. A minor character has even less "presence"; he is no more than a flicker. The sole function of El Viajero, ("The Traveler"), for example, is to be away; his presence is perceived only as the smell of his leather suitcases, which lingers on in chapters through which he has roamed.

The characters exist primarily as ideas, and their interest for the author and for the reader is primarily of a conceptual nature. They are copies of no one outside of the novel's subjective field. Having no external ties, they are to pass as concepts directly from the mind of the author to the mind of the reader.

The derivative nature of conventional literary characters is lampooned by Macedonio when he observes that the usual personage half-exists (is half-real) because half of him was taken from a real person; the person from whom the half was taken is left partially disabled:

> There are certain human beings walking the earth who have been partially used by a novelist and who feel a certain uneasiness with respect to their state of "being" alive. Some part of them is in the novel, fictionalized upon written pages, and it is hard to tell whether they exist more in the novel or out of it. (M, p. 41)

Macedonio's characters "derive," if the term be applicable, from the only source his Idealist aesthetic admits, from his own creative consciousness; they are responsible to it and to it alone. Noé Jitrik identifies a difficulty inherent in this form of creation. Jitrik's analysis contains several important insights into the nature and function of the characters in the novel of Belarte:

> This concerns his remark that it would be an

"authorial pretension" to select a character who was a "Genius" because this would presuppose that the author were one as well; a point which is well taken, because every imagination can be compared to the object which it is capable of imagining: besides, if the character is conceived in accordance with the norms of verisimilitude, this activates the system of identifications upon which verisimilitude rests— character-author, character-reader, reader-author. Being neither a Genius nor not a Genius—who can say? Macedonio thinks up a character called "Perhaps-a-Genius?," whose form is that of a conjecture-in-itself, an unverifiable possibility. That imprecise field extends to the author and includes him within it, since it was he who conceived of it in the first place. We notice then that there is one aspect of verisimilitude which remains in Macedonio, that of the identifications, but we also see that they operate upon conjectural models. He does not want to go on copying the real; his models reside in the realm of the imaginary and he conforms to its norms when he creates the Nonexistent Gentleman [el No-existente Caballero] and when he assembles his curious cast. . . .

But if to create a "Genius" character was an unacceptable "pretension," what about the creation of imaginary characters? This means following models which are also imaginary—let us remember that identification still exists—models which are found in that realm in which imagination gives them form. And if identification still exists, then the author is taking out of himself the stuff of his own imagination, his conjectural "substance." ("Destrucción de formas en las narraciones," p. 225)

Quizagenio, "Perhaps-a-Genius," an "unverifiable possibility," is the ideal character of Belarte. Neither a copy of a real model nor a purely arbitrary creation, he is a "copy of an imaginary model," who suggests an attribute (the function of the "identifications") precisely so that it may be contested. The referential circuit by which in verisimilitude we take the copy back to the model is permanently impaired; in the case of Quizagenio, unverifiability interrupts the circuit, other characters having a similar "breakdown" as an inherent part of their nature. Quizagenio, like the other characters, exists in a permanent state of contestation; his equivocal nature is permanently guaranteed.

"My aim is to create new objects which cannot be compared to any object in reality," Juan Gris once remarked. "My *Violin*, being a creation, need fear no competition"(quoted in Wylie Sypher, *Rococo to Cubism in Art and Literature*). This aim, nearly universal among the painters and poets of the avant-garde, has long been common to writers of fiction as well. Novelists since Flaubert have dreamed of the possibility of creating a fictive world not reducible to comparison with an external reality supposedly more authoritative than itself.* Gide complained that the trouble with the novel was that it had always been clinched to actualities (*cramponnée à la réalité*). In the *Journal des Faux-Monnayeurs* he speaks of the novelist's dilemma and divines a possible solution:

*"Ce qui me semble beau, ce que je voudrais faire, c'est un livre sur rien, un livre sans attache extérieure, qui se tiendrait de lui-même par la force interne de son style, . . . un livre qui n'aurait presque pas de sujet ou du moins le sujet serait presque invisible, si cela se peut," wrote Flaubert to Louise Colet on August 26, 1853.

D'une part, l'événement, le fait, la donnée extérieure; d'autre part, l'effort même du romancier pour faire un livre avec cela. Et c'est là le sujet principal, le centre nouveau qui désaxe le récit et l'entraîne vers l'imaginatif. Somme toute, ce cahier ou j'écris l'histoire même du livre, je le vois versé tout entier dans le livre, en formant l'intéret principal, pour la majeure irritation du lecteur.[4]

Gide contemplated this solution from the vantage point of a journal of his novel; Macedonio makes journal indistinguishable from "novel," as his title attests: "*Museo*" *de la novela de la Eterna*. "Museum," as Adolfo de Obieta observes, was not intended to suggest "glass cases faithful to an evolutive development, but a great storehouse of intentions, projects, materials, experiments, suggestions, in which one could find room for anything and everything" (Advertencia a *Museo de la novela de la Eterna*, p. 6). The "museum" could be said to hold the so-called novel of Eterna, as well as the partial contents of the President's projected novel. The entire project, however, museum and all, is encompassed within the subjective process of composition itself, which is neither completely real, nor completely fictional, but of an unverifiable status somewhere between the two; the "novel" is "unclinched" from externals.

The self-subsistence of the characters within this field is humorously affirmed by Macedonio when he rejects the application of Nicolasa Moreno to be a character in the novel. She is turned down because she wants to be allowed to leave at intervals to keep some food she left cooking on her stove from boiling over. These returns to her kitchen, Macedonio says, "would interrupt her performance in the work and I cannot provide for all these exits; in making

the world God erred when he forbade ubiquity" (M, p.
78). A figure who stands in relation to the world of
necessity cannot serve as a character, because that world is
alien to his fictional essence. The character cannot be
ubiquitous; he cannot perform his function as character,
Macedonio insists, if he is tied to the real world by the
need to watch a stove—or, presumably, to improve the
lot of miners or to overthrow the government. The
characters exist in and of the subjective field of the novel.

Within this field the characters all appear to allude to
some facet of the author's psyche. All, like Quizagenio,
are "unverifiable possibilities." While they allude to what
we know to have been persistent themes of the author's
imagination, the characters—Deunamor, el Presidente (an
author), el Autor, el Metafísico, Quizagenio, Eterna—do
not exactly meet the Proustian test of "sounding the
fundamental notes of the author's personality." The
referential system breaks down—as it is intended to—for
the characters resolutely both "are" and "are not" the
author. Each contains a drop of unreality sufficient to abort
the referential process. The characters are not simply
personified concepts—they have an emotional life, they
are tender and compassionate—but neither are they
"people." Macedonio has located them in a plane where
the reader is helpless to know how to deal with them.
Faced with an array of partially realized fictions, ultimately
irreducible to their supposed source, the reader must
finally give up his inferential, deductive habits and
abandon himself to the contemplation of a mode of being
in which coherence yields to freedom. To contemplate
the characters and to conclude that "they are this, but not
only this"; or "they are this, but not always this"; or
"they are this, but not necessarily this," is perhaps to
intuit new possibilities of individual freedom, one facet,

possibly, of the experience of *"conmoción conciencial"* Macedonio wanted for every reader: "I should like to be recognized as the first person to attempt to make full and efficient use of that prodigious instrument of ontological disruption, the character in a novel . . . " (M, p. 24).

If Macedonio can, through his stratagems, prevent the reader from associating his characters with accepted notions of personality, he can perhaps cause the reader to discern the fictive nature of the supposed boundaries of personality itself. The techniques of inhibiting this association are subtle, intricate: "sutil, muy paciente es el trabajo de desacomodar interiores, identidades" (M, p. 35). The character cannot behave so incomprehensibly that the reader dismisses him as mad. Purely arbitrary characters behaving with random absurdity—assuming that they could be realized—would not suffice for the operation of *desidentificación*. Macedonio, therefore, does not create "mad" characters; unpredictable behavior in a mad character is simple realism: "the incoherent and the absurd are the verisimiltude of madness. I do not provide mad characters but a mad text with the intention of convincing through art rather than through truth" (M, p. 6). The reader, in order to be properly affected, must be tempted into his old deductive habits by at least a minimum of recognizable personality. Picasso once noted, "You must always start with something. Afterward you can remove all traces of actuality. There is no danger anyway, for the idea of the object will have left its indelible mark" (quoted in Sypher, *Rococo to Cubism,* p. 268). The recognizable idea of the character, the indelible silhouette that remains in the mind of the reader, is what remains to Macedonio of the art of verisimilitude, as Jitrik pointed out: the identifications. "Removing all traces of actuality" is arduous. The reader's inclination to

personify fully the figures suggested by the author, to
create behind them satisfying psychological patterns, is
difficult to thwart.

Macedonio uses a number of devices to prevent the
spontaneous rounding out of the characters. One of these is
a kind of découpage; the characters are briefly glimpsed
and then abruptly snatched from view. This rapid cutting
away frustrates the reader who is looking for traditional
development, but it provides him with a vivid image of
the character, Macedonio believed that "characters and
events which are skillfully truncated are those which stick
in the memory" (M, p. 112). The evanescence of the
characters is a reminder, if one were needed, that they are
preeminently fictional:

> The reader believes himself a reader because the
> characters are characters for him both in the novel
> and in the prologues even though he has only brief
> and rather misty glimpses of them in scenes and
> episodes which are rapidly cut away. I believe that
> Eterna, Dulce Persona, Quizagenio, Deunamor will
> be unforgettable even though I have barely exposed
> them to the reading eye. . . . (M, p. 40)

Like Unamuno and Pirandello, Macedonio allows his
characters to debate freely their ontological status as
fictional beings. But whereas for Unamuno and Pirandello
the creation of the character by the author is a paradigm, a
reenactment of the creation of the individual by his Maker,
Macedonio's purpose is precisely to negate this paradigm.
Augusto Pérez, having been created in the image of his
author, can be extinguished with a single stroke. Author
and reader, having been created in the same mode, are
equally vulnerable when toward the end of the novel
Augusto becomes a shrieking *memento mori*:

God will stop dreaming of you! You will die, yes, you will die, even though you don't want to; you will die and all those who read my story will die, not a single one will be left! They are fictional beings just like me, exactly the same! Everyone will die, everyone, everyone, everyone. (Miguel de Unamuno, *Niebla,* Ch. 31)

Macedonio, who once referred to himself as Ningunamuno, moves in exactly the opposite direction. The characters are rigorously fictional, and the reader is not permitted to identify with their existential plight as creations of an Author. Having been created, they can be destroyed; their mode of existence is totally unlike that of the reader, who is "uncreated" (*increado*), and therefore immortal (NTV, p. 172). Their reason for being is precisely to manifest this difference: "There is only one form of nonbeing, that of the character of fiction, that of the imagined entity. The imaginer will never know nonbeing" (concluding sentence of *Museo*).

Another technique used by Macedonio for inhibiting the coherent development of character is the inclusion of contradictory elements in the characterization. Braque once remarked that in painting, "It is always desirable to have two notions, one to demolish the other" (quoted in Sypher, *Rococo to Cubism,* p. 265). Similarly, Macedonio's composite portrait of the President at once suggests a close identification with Macedonio himself and denies it.

I even experienced I kind of terror in writing it (the novel); because of this I had to say quite forcefully, "I am not the President." A devastating, dizzying sense of dread: for an instant, as I was creating the President and making him so much like

myself, I shook with fear, believing myself to be a life-
less character in my novel. (M, p. 191)

The technique, which prevents the reader from deducing
more about the character than is actually presented at a
given moment, seems to coincide with the process
Unamuno describes in his article "Pirandello y yo":
"Another of the confidences which this unknown donor
shared with Pirandello and with me was this way of
seeing and developing historical or fictional personalities in a lively flux of contradictions, like a whole series of
selves, like a spiritual river. The exact opposite of what is
called character in traditional dramaturgy" (p. 544).
Pirandello and Unamuno, however, introduce contradictions as a means of creating characters who are like the
variable selves of real people; Macedonio uses contradiction as Braque does, to sabotage the development of a
fixed pattern of identity.

A more disturbing confusion of identity is used by
Macedonio in the characterization of la Eterna. Eterna has
had previous existences as mysterious romantic heroine:
" . . . behold Eterna, who was called Lenore in Poe, and
Rebecca in *Ivanhoe,* and who can also be discerned in
Lady Rowena" (M, p. 59).

Macedonio, apparently speaking as himself, makes a
somewhat similar statement earlier in the book:

I think I resemble Poe very strongly, although
recently I have begun to imitate him a little;
I believe that I am another Poe. . . . It is not a resemblance, it is—who knows?—a reappearance.
As I wrote the poem "Elena Bellamuerte" I felt I
was Poe in sentiment and nevertheless the text does
not show any literary similarity.

I only make these affirmations in order to encourage the young reader to keep himself always on the defensive against the shipwreck-conviction—belief in a self whose fate is linked to the life and death of a body. (M, p. 37)

More is involved here, of course, than a mere confusion of identity; Macedonio in such passages is inviting the reader to consider alternative conceptions of personality, to question the fundamental Western assumption that personality is eternal, indestructible, not to be dissolved. Eterna's personality is a fabric of *personae* in the original, etymological sense, masks she can change at will, "through" which she "sounds" her roles.* But her being

*Heinrich Zimmer in *Philosophies of India* writes, "The term 'personality' is derived from the Latin *persona. Persona,* literally, means the mask that is worn over the face by the actor on the Greek or Roman stage. . . . The mask is what bears the features or make-up of the role, the traits of the hero or heroine, servant or messenger, while the actor behind it remains anonymous, an unknown being intrinsically aloof from the play. . . . Originally the term *persona* in the sense of 'personality' must have implied that people are only impersonating what they seem to be. The word connotes that the personality is but the mask of one's part in the comedy or tragedy of life and not to be identified with the actor. . . . . And yet the Western outlook—which originated with the Greeks themselves and was then developed in Christian philosophy—has annulled the distinction, implied in the term, between the mask and the actor whose face it hides. The two have become, as it were, identical. When the play is over the *persona* cannot be taken off; it clings through death and into the life beyond. The Occidental actor, having wholly identified himself with the enacted personality during his moment on the stage of the world, is unable to take it off when the time comes for departure, and so keeps it on indefinitely, for milleniums, even eternities —after the play is over" (pp. 236–37).

remains independent of her personae; she is Eterna—
eternal—precisely because she is not identical with the
fictive masks she wears. The notion of a permanently
constituted, fixed self is contested by the second text as
well: Macedonio not only felt *like* Poe, he felt he *was* Poe.
The suggestion seems to be that the persona is not grafted
to the body of he who wears it; in the course of a lifetime
one might conceivably assume any number of new
identities.

Underlying all of the pattern-making principles that
give rise to a conception of personality are deep-rooted
assumptions concerning the nature of time. As Macedonio
works to shake our belief in a real world and a real self
transcendent to consciousness, he must inevitably lead us to
question our analogous belief in real time. Like Husserl,
Macedonio distinguishes between time as it is experienced
by an individual and so-called real or cosmic time. Real
time is a nonentity, Macedonio notes, because no one has
experienced it. As Husserl puts it, "Just as a real thing or a
real world is not a phenomenological datum, so also
world-time, real time, the time of nature in the sense of
natural science including psychology as the natural science
of the psychical, is not such a datum."[5] For Macedonio,
real time is a mere word: "The absentees in the world are
the Self, Matter, Time, and Space: the genius of grammar
can substantivize them with a word which has the precise
effect of denying them as substances and as phenomena"
(NTV, p. 99). Duration for Macedonio, as for the phenomenologists, is constituted by modification of the contents
of consciousness: "Time is nothing, and two occurrences
or images between which there is no other occurrence or
image are immediate, although they are separated by,
absurdly speaking, so-called centuries" (NTV, p. 112).

Even historical time is an empty abstraction, Macedonio

says, for the idea of the *march of history* "exists only in historical writing, not in anyone's heart" (M, p. 126). An uncritical belief in historical time diminishes freedom, for the march of history is wedded to the idea of the inexorable working out of the laws of cause and effect. History with its assumption that the past determines the present, robs us of *now*. If we believe uncritically that past behaviour fashions present behaviour, freedom is an illusion; the present is relinquished before it arrives. Macedonio believes that we recapture the present in certain privileged moments of consciousness, instants of exaltation, love, enthusiasm: *Pasión*. At such moments we live a "continuum of present" in which anything is possible:

A present of passion, once we experience it, makes the future, the march of time, superfluous; the erroneous notion of the march of time exists only in historical writing, not in anyone's heart.

Passion gives no thought to situation, to time, to comparisons; for everyone there exists a continuum of present, the same present; what does not exist is that empty and never-attainable idea of Progress; there exists for everyone the perpetual opportunity for a new "launching," for sallying forth like Don Quixote. (M, p. 126)

Macedonio relies primarily upon two characters to convey the all-important insight that we have the power to be different from our past selves. They are Eterna and the President. Eterna, having led many lives, is not the sum of her past existences. Macedonio endows her with the magic power to *change the past* of other characters, to liberate them, metaphorically, from the constraints of past behaviour, from the necessity of being derived from their former selves. Eterna is thus a sign of infinite beginning. The President has place two signs at the entrance of his *estancia,* which is called "La Novela":

Leave ye here your pasts.
Cross my threshold and your pasts will not pursue ye. (M, p. 121)

The President, the author tells us, would be willing to be a historian, "not for the sake of restoring the past which History gave to Man, but for the sake of restoring the Present that History robs from him" (M, p. 208). "Presentism" is the name of the President's philosophy: "His watchword might be 'Live only in the Present, caring neither for history nor for future Progress.' For what we are is a beginning, a not-beginning-in-anyone-else, a not-originating-in, a not-resembling-anyone" (M. p. 208).

Like Eterna, the President is also a sign of infinite rebirth, of the euphorious, irrational affirmation, "There exists for everyone a perpetual opportunity for a new 'launching,' for sallying forth like Don Quixote."

Leo Spitzer once noted that "the lifeblood of the poetic creation is everywhere the same, whether we tap the organism at 'language' or 'ideas,' at 'plot' or at 'composition.' "[6] Whether we tap *Museo* at "theory," "characters," "structure," or "technique," we discover a similar dynamism. Every element bears the stamp of the President's ideal: "to begin, not-to-descend-from, not-to-derive-from, not-to resemble anyone else." Macedonio's aesthetic injunction to reject the copy was a reductive statement that distilled not only a theory of art, but a metaphysics, a psychology, and an ethics of freedom.

"Let art and all that is connected to it be absolutely free—its letters, its titles, the lives of those who revere it. Tragedy, Humor, and Fantasy should not be subject to the dictates of a governing Past; the idea should be to play and to renew without ceasing" (M, p. 47).

Characterization, then, in *Museo,* is projected out of the "work" and toward the reader. No characters are "given" to the reader from which he may draw inferences about enduring centers of personality. Characterization in the art of nonrealism is a process of *desidentificación:* it is the sum of the techniques by which the author brings about a breakdown in the usual circuit of reference, a circuit that can only reiterate a derivative view of personality Macedonio considered damaging. The equivocal characters of Belarte are indispensable agents in the process of breaking the reader's inferential habits and arousing his intuitive response. Since they serve this important function, and since it is through them that meaning is conveyed, we may conclude that the fragile figures who inhabit *Museo* are still preeminent structuring elements of the "novel," "novel" being by definition a text expressly designed to induce in the reader a radical experience of self-contestation.

Chapter V

Formal Aspects of the Novel of Belarte

"We are inveterate pattern makers," says William Gass in a recent essay on fiction, "imposing on the pure data of sense a rigorously abstract system. The novelist makes a system for us too, although his is composed of a host of particulars, arranged to comply with aesthetic conditions, and it both flatters and dismays us when we look at our own life through it. . . . "[1] Faced with a baffling "host of particulars"—a *Ulysses,* a *Cambio de Piel,* a *Paradiso*—the reader automatically begins to retrace the novelist's steps, attempting to discover the underlying pattern, the organic unity he is certain is there. Sufficiently motivated, he applies category after category until he discovers or thinks he discovers a pattern that informs the whole, a recognizable relationship between the fictional world created by the novelist and the world of his own experience. Such a discovery, although difficult, can be enormously rewarding, vindicating both the work in which the pattern

173

is discoverable and the world view to which it has reference.

But let us suppose that an author's purpose were *not* to vindicate either the reader's view of the world or his notion of a literary work, but to contest vigorously both of these conceptions. He might then hit upon the idea of writing his book in such a way that *no* underlying organic design were discoverable. What the reader of such a book might discover, presumably to his benefit, would not be a "flattering or dismaying pattern," but rather the ultimate inadequacy of all the categories he was trying to apply. Reading such a book would be a frustrating and disconcerting, but conceivably a liberating experience. Such a book, we believe, is Macedonio's *Museo*.

The book we are describing could not be a "work" of literature, since the distinguishing feature of the work is precisely its organic character, the coherent relationship of its various parts. The principles of composition of such a book would be the reverse of those of the work. Since these must now operate to disorganize rather than to organize the text, they would logically be such principles as discontinuity, incongruence, and digression. Obviously, such principles can only operate with respect to some anticipated or incipient design; one can only digress, for example, from some expected course of development. For this reason Macedonio, as he begins his experiment, gives us on the very first page of *Museo* the necessary frame of reference: his book will be "the first good novel" as opposed to "the last bad novel." As mentioned previously, Macedonio thought of publishing a particular "bad novel," his own *Adriana Buenos Aires,* to be specific, in the same volume with *Museo*. He eventually decided that the actual presence of this text was not essential; all that was really necessary for his purposes was the *idea* of the traditional novel as a familiar set of conventions against which he might work. The reader, whose mind was saturated with such novels, scarcely needed to have a specific example before his eyes.

The potential for contradiction between the two matrices—the "last bad novel" and the "first good one"— is an inexhaustible source of humor. In assaulting mimesis, Macedonio mimes, with the feigned earnestness of a master clown, the process of novel writing itself. With elaborate preparatory gestures, innumerable fresh starts, second thoughts, asides, and digressions, he makes as if to tell a story the true function of which is never to get told. We should note that Macedonio parodies not the bad novel (that would generate another novel), but the process of making it. His aim is not to produce another novel, but to effect a change in perception. It is not merely the *organum,* but the nature of the act of organizing that the parody calls into question.

The close kinship between Macedonio the novelist and Macedonio the analyst of the dynamics of humor and maker of conceptual jokes has been extensively studied in an illuminating book by Alicia Borinsky de Risler, *Macedonio y sus otros.* Little could be added to this excellent analysis. Macedonio quite consciously set out to produce a form of "serious prose" that might provide the kind of emotional release experienced in laughter:

My observation of the immediate power of humorous prose, of those poor written signs, to provoke the sudden convulsion of laughter, led me to consider whether the literature which I shall call serious . . . ought not to have an equally quick and sure effect, rather than the dubious results critics

G

ascribe to these works. ("Doctrina estética de la novela," p. 415)

His novelistic technique is modeled on his humorous praxis; the subtle mechanics of joke construction are applied to the narrative:

I think of both genres of prose, humorous and serious, as primarily intellectual in character, with the expectation of the concept and the expectation of the story being the two instruments for triggering another state of awareness unrelated to that which is expected. . . . (Ibid., p. 414)

The "bad" or traditional novel, then, is evoked as a set of literary conventions to be deliberately violated in the name of a higher good. In denying his "novel" the organic structure that characterizes the literary product of Western culture, Macedonio is contesting more than literary convention: he is assaulting an underlying belief that there are hidden realities which are the "designers of destiny." In making it impossible for the reader to discover a hidden design articulating the text, a unified and unequivocal pattern of meaning, Macedonio is undertaking a fundamental reorientation of the reader's pattern-seeking activity. There is considerable danger in this procedure. The author who violates convention, Kenneth Burke reminds us in *Counter-Statement*, violates a major tenet of form, "for he is disappointing the expectations of his audience; and form, by our definition, resides in the fulfillment of the audience's expectations" (p. 204). However worthy his aim, Macedonio will not be successful as an artist unless he can persuade us to accommodate our expectations to his methods. That is why aesthetic theory occupies such a privileged place in *Museo*. The prologues contain essential "lessons in aesthetic theory" whose clear, authoritative tone contrasts sharply with the tentative, equivocal character of the text as a whole. Whatever else Macedonio may contest, his aesthetic principles must stand firm, enabling the reader to readjust his expectations, or the experiment fails. Macedonio takes care that we understand what his aims and methods are and attempts to enlist us as allies of the project.

Form, then, presents a problem that Macedonio deals with by instructing the reader in aesthetic doctrine, thus manipulating to some extent his expectations. But subject matter presents a problem of a different order, one much more difficult to solve. The subject of a fictional work exerts a kind of polarizing force, becoming a center toward which all other aspects of the text are in some way directed. It is thus, in and of itself, one of the principal organizing elements of the "work."

Wells, alluding to the novels of Henry James, complained, "The thing that the novel is *about* is always there. It is like a church lit but with no congregation to distract you, with every light and line focussed upon the high altar."[2] Forster noted the same phenomenon in James's fiction: " . . . a pattern must emerge, and anything that emerged from the pattern was lopped off as wanton distraction" (*Aspects of the Novel*, p. 232). Macedonio, whose purpose it is to impede the formation of pattern, must remove subject matter from the high altar it has occupied in the traditional novel. The alternative to "the" subject, Macedonio suggests, is *any* subject:

I seriously believe that Literature is precisely the Belarte of artistically executing a subject discovered by someone else. This is the law of all Belarte, and it

means that the "subject" of art has no artistic value
in itself, or rather that execution is the entire value of
art. To classify subjects as better or worse, or as more
or less interesting, is to talk about ethics. To do the
aesthetic is to artistically execute any subject whatsoever. (M, p. 107)

Within the context of our usual ways of thinking about
the novel, this statement, even if purely rhetorical, is
puzzling. The novel we are familiar with makes its statement of meaning largely through the author's painstaking
selection of material. The intrinsic interest and value of this
material are an integral part of the novel's meaning. To
suggest that it could be chosen "by others," that is,
arbitrarily determined, is to ask us to consider a drastic
revision of our conception of meaning in fiction. If the
scales are tipped so violently in the direction of technique
that subject matter is regarded as virtually inconsequential,
if the formation of coherent thematic "centers" is dis-
credited, where *are* we to look for meaning? Is the novel of
Belarte *about* anything? Where is the "novel" located
within *Museo*?

In saying "execution is the entire value of art. To do
the aesthetic is to artistically execute any subject whatsoever," Macedonio is talking about more than the achievement of style understood as a kind of accessory veneer.
"Execution" signifies all that is done with the materials,
how they are *or are not* articulated, developed, formed into
recognizable designs. The meaning of Macedonio's text is
all that is signified by the disconcerting ways in which its
materials are utilized. Robbe-Grillet, speaking of a zebra, a
painting, a symphony, and a novel, observes that "it is in
their form that their meaning resides, their 'profound

signification,' that is, their content."³ This is what Macedonio means when he says,

> If what I call novel fails as such, my Aesthetic
> Theory will save the day: I am willing for it to be
> taken as a novel, as first-rate fantasy, as a stand-in for
> the novel. If the novel fails as such, it may be that my
> Aesthetics will serve as a good novel. (M, p. 40)

It is precisely at this point that the predictable charges
of "excessive preoccupation with form, failure to deal
with life," and so forth, can be met. The pursuit of
incoherence in *Museo* has no other aim than to effect a
particular change in the reader's responses to the experiences of life. *Museo's* meaning cannot be separated
from its intended effect upon the reader. The "matter" of
the novel, what it may be said to be "about," according to
Macedonio, is the reader himself:

> Author: You are what concerns me here, reader; you,
>   in your precarious presence, are my subject.
>   Everything else is simply a pretext to hold
>   you where my technique can reach you.
> Reader: Thank you. (M, p. 223)

The reader is the "human content" of *Museo,* and the
meaning of the book is the cumulative effect upon his
perception of a technique that "culminates in the use of
incongruities, to the point of forgetting the identity of the
characters and their continuity along with such things as
temporal sequence, causes before effects, etc. . . . " (M,
p. 38).

"The impulse to make 'gestalts' is universal, both in
experience and art," Philip Stevick observes in "The
Theory of Fictional Chapters." "As Kohler points out," he
continues, "built into every language are hundreds of

words which refer to this pattern-making faculty: brink, edge, beginning, end, close, piece, part, rest, remainder, proceeding, finishing, continuing, deviating, bending, retarding, and so on. Thus the impulse to enclose is a basic property of the mind. And consequently, the impulse to shape narratives into patterns is the ineluctable result of the human perceptions that lie at its basis" (*Theory of the Novel*, p. 173).

To observe the rudiments of design as they occur in *Museo*—the nature of beginning, development, and closure, whether of sentences, paragraphs, prologues or, of the whole—is to discover a fundamental consistency of the text. Macedonio works to reverse the terms of Stevick's formula, to alter perception by refusing to shape his narrative into a pattern. In *Museo* no emerging design is long tolerated at any level; clause by clause, the conjectural, the tentative, and the inconclusive prevail. The story all but disappears in the diffuse, essayistic passages which engulf it. The equivocal, self-contesting, interrogative nature of the text eradicates fixed points of reference. For Macedonio, as for certain other experimental novelists, the famous "concrete organizing principle" of the past, "the fixed pattern or object round which a universe would tend to crystallize and unfold itself,"[4] has become suspect.

Macedonio's quarrel is not with the principles of congruence, continuity, and so forth, which enable us to create systems, but with the inevitable inadequacy of the systems we create, with our tendency to take them for absolutes. Macedonio's character Quizagenio expresses succinctly the radical distrust of schema evidenced in every line of *Museo*: " . . . nothing of the essential Mystery of the All is clarified; no Mechanical or Psychological explanation will ever be adequate to reduce the Mystery in the slightest" (M, p. 173).

Quizagenio's conviction—which might be glossed, "no scheme is adequate to explain life; all schemes are suspect (including language)"—besides being the mark of Macedonio's modernity, is also the point at which his work can be articulated with that of a whole generation of Latin American novelists of which he was the unwitting precursor.

Robbe-Grillet, in his essay "On Several Obsolete Notions," notes that in the traditional novel "to tell a story well is to make what one writes resemble the prefabricated schemas people are used to, in other words, their ready-made idea of reality."* For Macedonio (as for Robbe-Grillet, although their tactics are very different), "telling a story well" means telling it so that the reader is incapable either of discovering or projecting such "prefabricating schemas." To do this is very difficult, for not only are we inveterate pattern makers, but we tend to make the same patterns again and again with the barest minimum of motivation. As we read, conditioned by hundreds of narratives read and remembered, we look for familiar constellations. Nathalie Sarraute in a well-known essay calls attention to the way in which readers tend to *create* a character in fiction even where none was intended. The process she describes applies as well to the reader's impulse to find designs.†

---

*"Bien raconter, c'est donc faire ressembler ce que l'on écrit aux schémas préfabriqués dont les gens ont l'habitude, c'est-á-dire á l'idée toute faite qu'ils ont de la réalité." *Pour un Nouveau Roman,* p. 30.

† "Le lecteur, en effect, même le plus averti, dès qu'on l'abandonne à lui-même, c'est plus fort que lui, typifie.

Il le fait—comme d'ailleurs le romancier, aussitôt qu'il se repose—sans même s'en apercevoir, pour la commodité de la vie quotidienne, à la suite d'un long entraînement. Tel le chien de

For even the most experienced reader, if left to his own devices, tends to create types; he simply can't resist it.

He does it, in fact—in the same way as the novelist, once he has begun to relax—without even noticing that he is doing it, for the convenience of everyday life and as a result of long practice. Like Pavlov's dog, in whom the tinkle of a bell stimulates the secretion of saliva, he creates characters at the slightest possible suggestion. As in the game of "statues," each one he touches turns to stone. They merely serve to swell in his memory the vast collection of inanimate figures to which, day in, day out, he is constantly adding and which, since he first learned to read, has constantly been growing as a result of the countless novels he has absorbed.[5]

Something analogous happens when we read of fictional events as well. We want to discover a casual relationship between happenings, to connect into orderly, justifying patterns the series of events that befalls the characters. The traditional novelist tries to make this easy for the reader, as Ford Madox Ford observes in his book on Conrad:

Before everything a story must convey a sense of inevitability: that which happens in it must seem

Pavlov, a qui le tintement d'une clochette fait sécréter de la salive, sur le plus faible indice il fabrique dès personnages. Comme au jeu des "statues", tous ceux qu'il touche se pétrifient. Ils vont grossir dans sa mémoire la vaste collection de figurines de cire que tout au long de ses journées il complète a la hate et que, depuis qu'il a l'age de lire, n'ont cessé d'enrichir d'innombrables romans.'
L'ère du soupçon, pp. 86–87.

to be the only thing that could have happened. Of course a character may cry; "If I had only acted differently how different everything would now be!" The problem of the author is to make his then action the only action that character could have taken.[6]

Even if the novelist did not strive for this effect of inevitability, the reader would, programmed as he is to do so by the thousands of pages of fiction he has ingested. Indeed, the traditional novelist counts heavily upon the reader's design-making ability. "A plot cannot be told to a gaping audience of cave men or a tyrannical sultan or to their modern descendant, the movie public. They can only be kept awake by 'and then—and then—.' They can only supply curiosity. But a plot demands intelligence and memory also," E. M. Forster points out in *Aspects of the Novel* (p. 130). The intelligent, memorious reader is expected to discover the hidden relatedness of separate events, to distinguish between real and apparent causes and to tie neatly together all the ends handed him.

But Macedonio has set out specifically to contest as a habit of both literature and life that "sense of inevitability" with which the traditional novelist is so complacent. His use of story is therefore entirely different from that of Balzac or Conrad or Galdós. Story interests him not as story but as a set of conventions against which he may work. Kenneth Burke, analyzing the appeal of conventional form, notes the attitude of the audience that "awaits" the "final Beethoven rejoicing of a Beethoven finale" before the first bar of music has even been played (*Counter-Statement,* p. 127). The most sophisticated reader, upon opening the cover of a novel, awaits a story. This expectation, together with an indispensable minimum of narrative material, enables Macedonio to have his way with the salivating reader. He rings the customary bells, but unlike Pavlov withholds the particular form of nourishment the reader thinks he needs, for Macedonio's purpose is not to reinforce habits of response but to break them. "Telling the story well" comes to be sustaining the expectation of a story; the reader's anticipation of the story takes the place of the story itself.

Macedonio repeatedly expressed his contempt for story *qua* story:

> Narrative and description are the horror of art. ("Doctrina estética de la novela," p. 413)

> It is academic fatuousness to believe in the Story. Aside from children, nobody believes in Stories. What *is* interesting is the theme or problem. . . . It is impossible for me to take a story seriously; the genre seems childish to me. (PR66, pp. 213–14)

A story was no more than a series of "and thens": "The 'ands' and the 'thens' make a narrative of any series of words; they baste everything together; they create 'suspense'" (Ibid., p. 214). What did interest Macedonio was the concept of story as it existed in the reader's mind—a complex of notions of beginning, development, and ending against which he could work comic marvels of disruption.

Macedonio out-Shandies Shandy in his manipulation of the element of structure called "beginning." The story, what Macedonio calls the *novel of the characters*, begins in this text of 50,000 words after a delay of nearly 25,000 words. At the end of the book's fifty-six prologues, at the threshold of the novel of the characters, two questions are posed by the author: "HAVE THE FOR-MER BEEN PROLOGUES? WILL WHAT FOLLOWS

BE A NOVEL?" Were the story that begins at this point synonymous with the "novel," both questions would of course be superfluous. But what we might call the "reader's novel" does not begin here; it begins, potentially, with the first prologue. As soon as the reader has formed a concept of "the good novel," he has begun to read it.

As might be expected, the characters' novel is the most ephemeral of stories. In accordance with the stipulations of Belarte, it contains:

1. No attempt to instruct nor to inform.
2. No appeal to the senses.
3. No finality except to be itself. ("Sobre 'Belarte,'" p. 43)

The "intrinsic appeal" of situation and setting is minimal; there is virtually no physical detail ("I term 'culinary' any kind of art which exploits the sensual for its intrinsic appeal and not for its potential for evoking emotion" [Ibid, p. 44]).

The rare inclusion of a strikingly "real" detail—allusion to the suicide of Alfonsina Storni, for example, or the mention that a certain event occurs on a Thursday in August in 1927—jars us into full awareness of the unreality of the fiction we are reading, just as the scraps of newsprint in a Cubist painting revealed the substantiality of the created world of the picture.

There is no conflict, no suspense, no drama in the characters' novel. Rather, we have a series of softly focused scenes that dissolve one into the other for no discernible cause. On a ranch called "La Novela" (the subject of "eternal litigation"), the characters have gathered to share a dreamlike existence—"a delightful life, free, refined, ever-changing, of deep affection and

shared affinities." The President acts as host, although the
property is not clearly his (the status of "La Novela"
being contested, like every other element of the narrative). He initiates the pleasant diversions that fill the days
of the guests, who view their residence in "La Novela"
as "a dream permanently untranslatable into reality. . . ."
The story is neither credible nor incredible, having
divorced itself from the exigencies of both of these modes
of narration. A chapter often begins with Dulce Persona
asking Quizagenio, "What do we have today in 'The
Novel'?" Quizagenio may reply, "Whatever you wish."
Macedonio achieves a feeling of improvisation, of free
invention; the characters have been cut loose from the
world of necessity. They belong to a mode of existence
Strindberg described in his remarkable prologue to "A
Dream Play":

> Everything can happen, everything is possible and
> likely. Time and space do not exist; on an insignificant
> basis of reality the imagination spins and weaves new
> patterns: a blending of memories, experiences, free
> inventions, absurdities, and improvisations.
>
> The characters split, double, redouble, evaporate,
> condense, scatter and converge. But one conscious-
> ness remains above all of them. He does not judge,
> does not acquit, simply relates.[7]

Despite the freedom and spontaneity of their existence,
an air of melancholy pervades the characters' novel. Its
source is the love-attachments of Quizagenio for Dulce
Persona, Dulce Persona for the President, and the President
for la Eterna. Macedonio considered the theme he called
"el Idilio-Tragedia" the only legitimate subject of
Belarte:

The only tragedy occurs without death, adultery, suicide, or infamy. There is only one eminent "subject" for art, and it is the idyll-tragedy of Love and its cessation in Oblivion, without death, because of the imperfection or the exhaustion of feeling: for those who have once loved to go on living having forgotten each other is a greater tragedy than death. In this example the plot, the "subject" does not exist. ("Doctrina estética," p. 414)

The last sentence explains the admissibility of the theme: all that remains of "incident" is an attenuated silhouette in memory—the hope or promise of what will never be, or—the supreme example—the tragic dissolution of emotion in oblivion.

Very little actually happens in the characters' novel: Macedonio confesses that he would have preferred to discover for his "novel" "the region where nothing happens, or, as it is called, 'Lion Country' " (M, p. 105). Not yet in "Lion Country," the reader witnesses a few vestigial incidents, notably the remarkable Conquest of Buenos Aires by the characters, who initiate a poetic campaign to beautify the city, to rescue it from the official, utilitarian ugliness that has invaded it.

But the greatest portion of the characters' novel is not incident but is of the same discursive, essayistic character as the prologues themselves. Various types of literary texts are interpolated into the characters' novel: diaries, letters, poems, and a short story are included, as well as the notes for the President's novel. Reading and commenting on these texts is the chief activity of the guests at "La Novela." Macedonio, we recall, admired in Cervantes the technique of engaging the characters in literary debate. The passage of the *Quijote* in which the characters

discuss the *Quijote* of Avellaneda was, according to
Macedonio, the inauguration of "technical or conscious
prose" ("Doctrina estética de la novela," p. 416).

In *Museo*, as in the *Quijote*, these discussions lend a
forum for the legitimate debate of conflicting views on
literature, as well as providing a means of access to the
metaphysical questions raised by the novels. Inevitably,
fictional characters who discuss another fiction are
unconsciously analyzing their own ontological status. The
reader absorbed in the delicious irony of their statements
is himself caught up in the ontological confusion—a
"liberating experience," in Macedonio's view (*de una
fecundidad conciencial liberadora*).

The ideal permutation of *Museo*, Macedonio tells us in
one of the concluding paragraphs of the book, would
greatly multiply the possibilities of contrasting many
textures of actuality and fiction:

> Here I insist that my theory of the novel could best
> be executed in a novel in which several persons had
> gathered to write a novel together, so that they, the
> reader-characters—readers of the other novel and
> characters in this one—would constantly stand out as
> real persons because of the contrast between them-
> selves and the figures and images they were reading
> about.
>
> Such a plot, made up of some characters who were
> both reading and being read and others who were
> merely being read, were it systematically developed,
> would comply with the demands of the theory. . . .
> Plot for a double novel. (M, p. 236)

Macedonio leaves the execution of this suggested
version of *Museo* to any future reader who may wish to

undertake the project. But in "his own version" of *Museo*, he thoroughly exploits the principle involved— the deliberate juxtaposition of contrasting modes of existence. Fictional characters invade the essays and receive instruction in aesthetic theory; William James appears in a series sandwiched between Eterna and Deunamor; the reader is asked to turn his back and read over his shoulder for a moment because Dulce Persona wants to change her dress; the author is burned by a hot ash from a reader's cigarette. In a thousand ways we are required to consider how it is we actually differ from each fictional being whose image has lodged itself in our consciousness.

Part of this play of contrasting planes is Macedonio's insistent use of the technique of authorial intrusion. Though the technique has a long tradition, it was not generally admired in the nineteenth century. By and large, the clash of contrasting frames of reference struck the nineteenth-century reader as unpleasant and decidedly inartistic. Sir Walter Scott censured writers who like Ginés de Pasamonte thrust their heads out from behind the curtain to explain what they are doing, for "they remind us that we are perusing a work of fiction, and that the beings with whom we have been conversant during the perusal are but a sort of evanescent phantoms, conjured up for our amusement."[8] In *The Art of Fiction* (1884) Henry James wrote that for the writer "to give himself away" ... "must bring tears to the eyes of those who take their fiction seriously." Trollope's want of discretion in this particular seems to him "a betrayal of a sacred office ... a terrible crime," which shocks him as much in Trollope as it would in Gibbon.

The farther we move away from mimesis, the greater our potential for enjoying the contradiction between real and created worlds. The twentieth century, it scarcely needs to be noted, finds this dissonance exhilarating. The contrast of textures of actuality and art seems to the modern audience to augment the substantiality of both worlds. Braque, for example, liked to take his paintings out into the fields "to have them meet things," certain that his representation could hold its own against the natural world from which he had excluded it" (Sypher, *Rococo to Cubism*, p. 300). When Gertrude Stein remarked that the portrait Picasso had painted of her did not resemble her at all, he replied simply, "It will." *Una fecundidad conciencial liberadora.*

Macedonio frequently "thrusts his head out from between the curtains" and keeps up a running commentary on his activity as author: "We have here a letter which no great writer of a great novel such as this one would ever have drafted in such sloppy, tear-jerking, windy language, we might as well admit it" (M, p. 158). These ironic intrusions, although frequently very funny, serve the serious purpose of deliberately notifying the reader that "the beings with whom we have been conversant are a sort of evanescent phantoms" whose mode of existence is not ours. Diametrically opposed to James, Macedonio would consider it a "betrayal of sacred office" (if he spoke so solemnly) *not* to dis-illusion the reader:

There is one reader I cannot become reconciled to: the reader who covets that which all novelists—to their discredit—give him: Hallucination. I want the reader to be constantly aware that he is reading a novel and not witnessing living—not watching "life." The moment the reader falls into Hallucination, the ignominy of Art, I have lost, not gained a reader. (M, p. 39)

All the techniques we have been discussing, in fact, share the common purpose of shifting attention away from a "hallucinatory" absorption in the materials themselves and toward the conceptual aspect of the text—that is, toward the question of its problematical existence as a fictional creation.

The anticipated development of the novel never occurs, but is systematically, comically defeated. The gratuitous adventure of the characters ceases as inexplicably as it began—without conflict, without drama, and without resolution. The curious cast of characters that has briefly resided in "La Novela" simply disperses. Try as he will, the reader cannot mobilize the elements of this vestigial story or of the text as a whole into any stable configuration. Like the flamingo-mallets, soldier-wickets, and hedgehog-balls with which Alice valiantly attempted to play croquet, the various elements of the text refuse to cooperate to play the game according to the rules: *Museo* is carefully constructed so that all of its pieces cannot fall nicely into place. In his refusal to allow the text to cohere around any discernible axis, Macedonio has implicitly posed a question about the nature of the coherence we attribute to our usual experience of life. In refusing to allow his text to assume the expected organic structure of a work of literature, in effectively preventing it from reflecting a reality supposedly more authoritative than itself, Macedonio challenges a whole chain of cultural assumptions leading back to the one he considered most damaging of all: the notion that behind the world of appearances there lies a reality more substantial and more authoritative than the world of experience.

Any number of contemporary novelists have assaulted this notion, like Macedonio, through the deliberate pursuit of incoherence, as Leo Bersani notes:

I have suggested that the very notion that phenomena reflect or correspond to a reality behind them
prejudices both our sense of what is possible and our
reading of what we see. The understandable if not
entirely logical assumption implicit in the belief in
realities deeper than appearances is that if behavior is
derivative, it is also intelligible. A personality explains
an individual's acts; an artist's life provides the key to
his work's coherence; or the obsessive themes of his
imagination organize the artist's work into a unified
design. The pursuit of incoherence in modern art can
therefore be thought of as the most dramatic aspect of
an attack against art's complicity with cultural myths
about hidden realities as the designers of experience.
(*Balzac to Beckett*, p. 12)

The elements of *Museo*, intentionally, do not converge
toward a fixed center; movement is not centripetal but
centrifugal, as Macedonio himself declares:

Let us construct a spiral so full of twists and turns
that the very wind grows weary in blowing through
it and comes out dizzy and disoriented; once and for
all let us construct a novel that is not a clear, faithful,
realistic copy. Art is either superfluous, or it has
nothing to do with Reality. Only in the latter case is
it real, just as the elements of reality are not copies of
anything else. (M, p. 109)

But freedom is never absolute. Invention is subject, at
the very least, to the conditions of human existence. The
orbit of any human project is conditioned by the facts of
corporality and mortality. Leo Bersani points out,

At the very least, particular acts are performed by

bodies, and the chemistry and mere mass of our bodies preclude any definition of freedom as pure, unconstrained invention. Similarly, as long as we cannot conceive of not dying, the fact of time which, whatever else it may lead to, must also lead to death, provides a permanent theme for every life to which every act, however, evasively, remains responsible. The body and mortality are thus the centers in life which create the magnetic field from which no human project has yet escaped. (*Balzac to Beckett,* p. 18)

And yet, as if drawn to project his ideal of total freedom to the limit of conceivability, Macedonio hints at a trajectory that would escape even the "magnetic field" of earthly existence. In "Novelas en 'La Novela,' " one of the last chapters in *Museo,* we survey the novel projected by the President, a novel the President says he "intends to write but will never actually *write.*" The President's is an original conception of the novel, called *"novelismo de la conciencia"* or *"novela sin mundo."* The characters are not physical persons but fields of consciousness:

The characters, which are not physical persons but minds, were people from life—they have lived in the Dualism or World; they live now in the universe of mental occurrence, which is absolutely deterministic with an intermental determinism: every time an intense state occurs in someone, it passes to all the others; why does it affect the others?; these "whys" do not exist: these are the facts and that is all there is to it. (M, pp. 195–96)

The characters, who lack "physical bodies, sense organs,

cosmos," communicate directly with one another without recourse to words. Their Idealist existence has not the slightest need of contact with the physical universe: The purpose of such a novel is not merely to assure the reader that he is immortal, but what is even more difficult, to make his immortality intellectually conceivable: "In other words, the effect which this kind of novel writing hopes to achieve is that of delineating in the reader's mind a conception of pure being [*el mero ser conciencial*], without a world, as an intelligible possibility" (M, p. 197).

A whole cast of phantasmal characters is named, including:

Beauty-in-Death: who left so that there might be more love, so that love might be exalted.

Unforgettable: who refuses to be forgotten even in death.

Lost One: who knows not who she is, nor who she was, nor why she is here, nor who she was before, nor what she will become, nor whether the one who perceives is really she or someone else.

Amneses: without a past. What happened yesterday did not occur.

Retroante: changes pasts. Some ask him for a happy past. others, to change their pasts, so that they may become convinced that they led lives other than the ones they led.

Mnemonia: she consists entirely of memory; she has no real being or life. But she has a perfect memory: there is no detail, however fleeting or insignificant, that she cannot recall or relive.

Eterna: she does not know death. . . . Maximum intensity of awareness.

Deunamor: awaits Beauty-in-Death. He must obtain
her spiritual resurrection and prove to her that
there is no greater happiness than the plenitude of
the spirit in a present—that is to say eternal—
moment of passion. (M, pp. 198-99)

Since the President does not himself enjoy the mode of
existence of his characters, that is, since he still pertains to
the physical world to which his readers also belong, he
must of necessity use *words* in writing his novel. There is
no way around this, for although the characters have no
use for words, the readers still need them: "So long as the
author has a body and writes for readers who have bodies,
as he writes the novel of the group of spirits [*el grupo
conciencial*], he will use words; although those in the
group do not use words, the readers still need them"
(M, p. 200).

The use of language in the *novela sin Mundo* is necessarily
governed by the extraordinary nature of the subject
matter. The chapter contains a kind of *preceptiva* for the
writing of such a text, a series of brief axiomatic statements, some of which, because of their emphasis on
compression, allusion, and the importance of metaphor,
recall the aesthetic creeds of Argentine Ultraism:

Exploitation of nearly forgotten meanings of words
and their irregular associations. To bring into play or
make use of a certain object or nucleus of associations
such as: the tick-tock of the clock on a bedside table—
the whistle of the wind—thresholds—a glove—the
anger of a rose—someone closing a piano—a dangling
button—the challenge of a carnation— . . .
Exploitation of the joys and sorrows of family life.
The mnemonic context of the present: what

position does a present, any present, occupy?: I get
up today and I think yesterday. . . .
   Scenes: With the laughter of a rose—With the
tick-tock of a little clock under the pillow—The
breathing of a sleeping person—Glances that meet.
(M, p. 200)

The notes also include a digest of the metaphysical notions
which the practitioner of *"el novelismo inter- o intra-
conciencial"* must impart to his readers. In short, Macedonio has provided the imagination with everything
necessary, a complete "kit," so to speak, for the creation of
the *novela sin mundo*.

We recognize that these "notes on the novel" are by
no means the exclusive property of the fictional President.
Not only does the cast of characters include several of the
characters who appear in Macedonio's *Museo de la novela
de la Eterna,* but the mode of existence of the characters in
the President's novel is identical with Macedonio's own
conception of existence after death as outlined in letters
to Gómez de la Serna and elsewhere. These few pages may
be the most important in *Museo,* the moment for which
the entire conceptual obstacle course is intended to
prepare us. For exactly as the the President intends, the
image of "el mero ser conciencial sin mundo, como
posibilidad inteligible" remains indelibly delineated in the
reader's mind.

   Gide remarks in the *Journal of "The Counterfeiters,"* [9]

The difficulty lies in not constructing the rest of my
novel as a prolongation of the lines already traced.
A perpetual upheaval; each new chapter must pose a
new problem, be an overture, a new direction, a new

impulse, a forward plunge—of the reader's mind. But the reader must leave me as a stone leaves the slingshot. I am even willing that, like a boomerang, he should come back and strike me.*

Macedonio's intent is similar to Gide's; the reader of *Museo* is propelled forward in three stages of acceleration: the prologues, the novel of the characters, and the President's projected novel. It is inevitable that the reader "leave the author's hand" and continue of his own momentum, following a trajectory that leads out of the book. The ending of *Museo*, quite logically, does not close off but opens out the narration.

The reader who as he reads anticipates a final solution is looking for what art ought not to give, Macedonio insists (M, p. 72). The kind of narration that leads to a "final solution" is itself the epitome of the closed system which it is Macedonio's purpose to contest. Such a narration is impelled by what Kenneth Burke has called "syllogistic progression": a given set of premises drives toward a particular conclusion. It was no surprise for Poe, for example, to learn from Dickens that Godwin had written "Caleb Williams" *backwards*, receding from an impressive final effect toward a beginning in the precise series of logical steps that would make the ending possible. Poe himself is certain that "it is only with the dénouement constantly in mind that one can give a plot its

---

*Ne pas établir la suite de mon roman dans le prolongement des lignes déjà tracées; voilá la difficulté. Un surgissement perpétuel; chaque nouveau chapitre doit poser un nouveau problème, être une ouverture, une direction, une impulsion, une jetée en avant—de l'esprit du lecteur. Mais celui-ci doit me quitter, comme la pierre lancée quitte la fronde. Je consens même que, boomerang, il s'en revienne frapper contre moi. (*Journal des Faux-Monnayeurs*, p. 74).

indispensable air of consequence, of causation, by making the incidents and especially the tone at all points tend toward the development of the intention."[10] Such an obsessive concern with producing a final revelation, solution, or effect is of course the antithesis of the creative freedom to which Macedonio aspires.

Most modern novelists, having rebelled against the obviousness of syllogistic development in its simple form, and rejecting the romantic charge of the dramatic final revelation, use more sophisticated tactics. Almost as a matter of course, they shatter the too easily identifiable pattern, shuffling the fragments as if they were a deck of cards, so that the reader may have the pleasure of discovering what has been hidden for him in "a host of particulars." But this variation of syllogistic progression provides no more than an illusion of freedom; all of the necessary pieces must be provided and they must *fit*.

But art, as Macedonio conceives it, ought not to give solutions. It is the writer's duty *not* to feed the reader's habit of conceiving the world as a *sign* of the truth, and experience as a mystery he must solve. His entire aesthetic program is designed to contest these habits of mind:

> The present aesthetic project is a provocation to the realist school, a program of total discreditation of the truth or reality of what the novel relates, a complete surrender to the truth of Art—intrinsic, unconditional, self-authenticating. It is in Art that I make my challenge to Verisimilitude, to that deformed intruder in Art, Authenticity. My challenge renders ridiculous anyone who embraces a Dream demanding all the while that it be Real. It culminates in the use of incongruities, to the point of forgetting all about the identity of the characters and their continuity along

with such things as temporal sequence, causes before effects, etc., *for which reason I invite the reader not to stop to try to untangle absurdities or rationalize contradictions but to allow himself to be carried along by the emotional impetus which the reading of this novel gradually arouses in him.* (M, p. 38) [emphasis added]

If the novel is to achieve the reorientation of perception that Macedonio intends, it cannot "conclude," if conclusion is understood in the Aristotelian sense of the inexorable completion of a design. But this is certainly not to say that the ending of the novel must be abrupt, arbitrary, or unsatisfying.

Macedonio, in fact, ends his "novel" with consummate grace, satisfying perfectly the nearly impossible requirements of his own rigorous doctrine. Final closure of the text is prevented in the same way in which the completion of design has been inhibited throughout the book. An ending is provided and immediately contested: it is not the *best* ending, we are told; furthermore, what we have been reading all along is not even the best *version* of the novel. A better version is briefly outlined. The book closes with a final prologue, in which the reader himself is fully authorized for the task of writing a new version of *Museo de la novela de la Eterna:*

To Whoever Would Like to Write This Novel
I leave an open book: perhaps it will be the first "open book" in literary history; that is, the author, wishing it were better, or at least good, and convinced that its mutilated structure is a dreadful discourtesy to the reader, but also convinced that the book is rich in suggestions, hereby authorizes any future writer whose temperament and circumstances favor intense

labor to freely edit it, with or without mentioning my
name. The task will not be small. Delete, amend,
change, but, if possible, let something remain. (M, p.
236)

The open-endedness of Museo is its final statement of
meaning, the sign and seal of the essential dynamism of
of the text. Like the Cubist object, Macedonio's "novel,"
theoretically at least, is not to have an absolute form, but
is to persist in the infinite permutations its lines suggest.
In the novel of Belarte, Macedonio has created a vehicle
capable not merely of enunciating but of signifying
through its form the fundamental insight of his Idealism,

Plainer than Day
   is Being,
the fullness of our being,
everlasting,
individual and memorious,
without beginning, without break, without end.
                                        (NTV, p. 75)

For Macedonio, the usual aesthetic product of our
culture, the work of art, could not but suggest finitude;
his aim was to create a sign of eternality. To this end he
struggled to realize the protean text-in-the-making, the
"novel" that might signify through its dynamism the
eternal and unconditioned activity of the mind. "The
imaginer will never know nonbeing" are his last words
to us (M, p. 237).

Notes

INTRODUCTION

1. Jorge Luis Borges, Address given at the funeral of Macedonio Fernández, reprinted in *Sur*, III–IV (1952), p. 147.
2. Juan Ramón Jiménez, "Lado de Macedonio Fernández," *La corriente infinita: critica y evocación* (Madrid" Aguilar, 1961), p. 186.
3. "El evangelio según M.F.," *Primera Plana*, 253, 31 October 1967, p. 66.
4. Emir Rodríguez Monegal, *El Boom de la novela latinoamericana* (Caracas: Editorial Tiempo Nuevo, 1972), p. 80.
5. Ramón Gómez de la Serna, "Silueta de Macedonio Fernández," *Sur*, VII, No. 28 (1937), p. 75.
Antonio Pagés Larraya, "Macedonio Fernández," 20 *Ficciones argentinas* 1900–1930 (Buenos Aires: EUDEBA, 1963), p. 71.
Carlos Fuentes, *La nueva novela hispanoamericana* (Mexico: Editorial Joaquin Mortiz, 1969), p. 24. (The other "founders" are Horacio Quiroga, Roberto Arlt and Felisberto Hernández).
Bernardo Canal Feijóo, "Teoría de Macedonio Fernández," *Davar*, No. 1, 1945, p. 67.
H.A. Murena, "Le premier Argentine maître de son propre génie," *Les Lettres Nouvelles*, July–August–September, 1965, p. 76.
6. The views and reminiscences of Eduardo González Lanuza, Ilka Krupkin and Bernardo Canal Feijóo were expressed to me in personal interviews in Buenos Aires in the spring of 1971. Lisardo

Zía's statement can be found in his article "Instantánea de Macedonio Fernández." *La Gaceta del Sur,* No. 8, Oct.–Nov. 1928.

7. "Jorge Luis Borges evocó a Macedonio Fernández," *La Razón,* 28 April 1962.

8. Rodolfo Alonso, "A nosotros Macedonio Fernández," *Norte* (Amsterdam), 7, No. 6, Nov.–Dec. 1966, p. 121.

I. THE LONG GESTATION OF A NOVELIST

1. Noé Jitrik, "La 'novela futura' de Macedonio Fernández," pp. 30–70. This seminal study of Macedonio's theory of the novel is indispensable to any serious analysis of *Museo de la novela Eterna.* Chapters 3, 4, and 5 of this study contain numerous references to Jitrik's illuminating perceptions.

2. I am indebted for this information to Luis Soler Cañas, who discovered the long-forgotten *El Progreso* articles and was gracious enough to share them with me in 1971.

3. Ricardo Hogg, *Guía biográfica* (Buenos Aires: Peuser, 1904), p. 75.

4. Quoted by Amaro Villauneva in "El fiscal Dr. Macedonio Fernández, sueño," *Argentina Libre,* 1941.

5. *El desterrado: vida y obra de Horacio Quiroga* (Buenos Aires: Losada, 1968), p. 163.

6. Juan Ramon Jiménez, *La corriente infinita* (Madrid: Aguilar, 1961), pp. 181, 186.

7. Reprinted in Ricardo Victorica, *Crítica baladí* (Buenos Aires, 1942), p. 165.

8. Hector René Lafleur, Sergio Provenzano, and Fernando P. Alonso, *Las revistas literarias argentinas* 1893–1967, Edición Corregida y Aumentada (Buenos Aires: Centro Editor, 1968), p. 63.

9. Mario Trejo, "Introducciones a Macedonio Fernández," *El Nacional,* 4 January 1959.

10. *Escritores representativos de América* (Madrid: Gredos, 1957), II:202.

11. Rene Wellek and Austin Warren, *Theory of Literature,* (N.Y.: Harcourt, Brace and World, 1956), p. 156.

II. A COMBATIVE IDEALISM

1. Quoted by William James in *Some Problems in Philosophy* (New York: Greenwood Press, 1968), pp. 121–22.
2. David Ballin Klein, *Encyclopaedia Britannica*, 1962, s.v. "Dreams."
3. We can postulate in the mind of an individual (or of two individuals who do not know each other, but in whose minds the same process is at work), two identical moments. Having postulated this equality, it is natural to ask: Are not those identical moments the same moment? Is not the repetition of a single term sufficient to confound and put to rout the entire temporal series? *Otras inquisiciones* (Buenos Aires: Emecé, 1960), pp. 243–4.

III. THEORY OF THE NOVEL: BELARTE CONCIENCIAL

1. For a detailed analysis of this relationship, see Ian Watt, *The Rise of the Novel: Studies in Defoe, Richardson and Fielding* (Berkeley and Los Angeles: University of California Press, 1967).
2. "Doctrina estética de la novela" was published by Germán Arciniegas in *Revista de las Indias*, July 1940: 412–17. "Para una teoría de la humorística" appears in PR44, pp. 185–258, and in *Teorías (Obras completas, vol. 3).*
Other texts interesting in this connection: "Sobre 'Belarte,' poesía o prosa," a letter from M. F. to Pedro Juan Vignale, in *Poesía* (June 1933): 43–44; "Fragmento sobre la metáfora," a letter from M. F. to Francisco Luis Bernárdez, in *Libra* (Bs. As.), Winter 1929, p. 83; "Leccioncita de psicoestética," in PR66, pp. 137–38; "Correspondencia de M. F. a Ramón Gómez de la Serna," transcribed and with a comment by Alicia Borinsky de Risler, in *Revista iberoamericana*, January–March 1970: 111–23.
3. Rodríguez Monegal, *El Boom de la novela latinamericana*, p. 80.
4. *La realidad y los papeles* (Madrid: Aguilar, 1967), p. 152.

5. "El estilo de la revolución," in *Literatura hispanoamericana,* edited by Enrique Anderson Imbert and Eugenio Florit (New York: Holt, Rinehart and Winston). 2 vols, II, p. 450.

6. Alan W. Watts, "Western Mythology, Its Dissolution and Transformation," in *Myths, Dreams and Religion,* ed. Joseph Campbell (New York: Dutton, 1970), p. 11.

7. "Nothing is more clear than that every plot, worth the name, must be elaborated to its dénouement before anything is attempted with the pen. It is only with the dénouement constantly in mind that we can give a plot its indispensable air of consequence, of causation, by making the incidents, and especially the tone at all points, tend to the development of the intention." Edgar Allan Poe, "The Philosophy of Composition," in *Representative Selections,* ed. Margaret Alterton and Hardin Craig, rev. ed. (New York: Hill and Wang, 1969), p. 365.

8. In the 1960 edition of *Literatura hispanoamericana* (New York: Holt, Rinehart and Winston), Macedonio is termed *"loco"* and his work is described as *"ilegible digresión"* (p. 501). In the 1970 revision of the anthology, it is stated that "[Macedonio] escribió poco porque no le interesaba la literatura" II, p. 155. The word *"loco"* has been changed to *"anormal"* in the revised edition.

IV. CHARACTER AND SELF-IMAGE IN BELARTE

1. Hippolyte Adolphe Taine, *History of English Literature* (New York: Colonial Press, 1900), 1:5.

2. From Freud's introductory lectures, quoted by Eric Fromm in *Zen Buddhism and Psychoanalysis* by D. T. Suzuki, Eric Fromm, and Richard De Martino (New York: Harper and Row, 1970), p. 82.

3. *Otras Inquisiciones,* p. 69.

4. André Gide, *Journal des Faux-Monnayeurs* (Paris: Gallimard, 1927), p. 45.

5. Edmund Husserl, *The Phenomenology of Internal Time-Consciousness,* (Bloomington: Indiana U. Press, 1964), p. 23.

6. Leo Spitzer, *Linguistics and Literary History* (Princeton, 1948), quoted by Richard M. Ohmann in "Prolegomena to the

Analysis of Prose Style" in *The Theory of the Novel*. ed. Stevick, p. 208.

V. FORMAL ASPECTS OF THE NOVEL
OF BELARTE

1. William H. Gass, *Fiction and the Figures of Life* (New York: Knopf, 1970), p. 71.
2. In "Boon," quoted by Forster, *Aspects of the Novel*, p. 232.
3. Alain Robbe-Grillet, *For a New Novel: Essays on Fiction*, trans. Richard Howard (New York: Grove Press, 1965), p. 43.
4. Jean-Pierre Richard, *L'Univers imaginaire de Mallarmé* (Paris, 1961), quoted by Leo Bersani in *Balzac to Beckett*, p. 17.
5. *The Age of Suspicion* (New York: Braziller, 1963), pp. 67–68.
6. Ford Madox Ford, *Joseph Conrad: A Personal Remembrance* (1924, rpt. N.Y.: Octagon Bks., 1971) pp. 218–219.
7. *A Dream Play and Four Chamber Plays*, trans. Walter Johnson (Seattle: University of Washington Press, 1973), p. 19.
8. Sir Walter Scott, "Tobias Smollett," in *Lives of the Novelists* (1827).
9. *The Counterfeiters with the Journal of "The Counterfeiters"* the novel translated by Dorothy Bussy and the journal translated by Justin O'Brien, (N.Y.: Alfred A. Knopf, 1962), p. 409.
10. Edgar Alan Poe, "The Philosophy of Composition," in *Representative Selections*, Margaret Alterton and Hardin Craig (New York: Hill and Wang, 1969), p. 365.

List of Works Consulted

Works by Macedonio Fernández

No toda es vigilia la de los ojos abiertos: arreglo de papeles que dejó un personaje de novela creado por el arte, Deunamor, el No-existente Caballero, el estudioso de su esperanza. Buenos Aires: Gleizer, 1928.

Papeles de Recienvenido. Buenos Aires: Proa, 1929.

Una novela que comienza. Prologue by Luis Alberto Sánchez. Santiago de Chile: Ercilla, 1941.

Papeles de Recienvenido. Continuación de la nada. Prologue by Ramón Gómez de la Serna. Buenos Aires: Losada, 1944.

Muerte es Beldad. Comment by Marcos Fingerit. La Plata: Ediciones de Marcos Fingerit, 1942.

Poemas. Prologue by Natalicio González. Illustrations by Carlos Coffeen Serpa. Mexico: Guarania, 1953.

Macedonio Fernández. Anthology. Selection and prologue by Jorge Luis Borges. Buenos Aires: Ediciones Culturales Argentinas, 1961.

Papeles de Macedonio Fernández: Antología de sus escritos. Selected and with a prologue by Adolfo de Obieta. Buenos Aires: Eudeba, 1965.

Codear fuera a Kant es lo primero en metafísica. Prologue by Ilka Krupkin. Limited edition. Buenos Aires: Colombo, 1966.

Papeles de Recienvenido. Poems, tales, miscellany. Selected and with an introduction by Adolfo de Obieta. Buenos Aires: Centro Editor de América Latina, 1966.

No toda es vigilia la de los ojos abiertos. Buenos Aires: Centro Editor de América Latina, 1967.

Museo de la Novela de la Eterna. Buenos Aires: Centro Editor de América Latina, 1967.

Selección de escritos. Buenos Aires: Centro Editor de América Latina, 1968.

Cuadernos de todo y nada. Buenos Aires: Ediciones Corregidor, 1972.

Manera de una psique sin cuerpo. Prologue by Tomás Guido Lavalle. Barcelona: Tusquets Editor, 1973.

Obras completas, 10 vols. Buenos Aires: Ediciones Corregidor, 1974– .

Projected Series: I, *Papeles antiguos;* II, *Epistolario;* III, *Teorías;* IV, *Papeles de Recienvenido y Continuación de la nada;* V, *Adriana, Buenos Aires;* VI, *Museo de la novela de la Eterna;* VII, *Poemas, relatos y misceláneas;* VIII, *No toda es vigilia la de los ojos abiertos;* IX, as yet untitled; X, *Ensayos sobre Macedonio Fernández.*

General

Barrenechea, Ana Maria. "Macedonio Fernández y su humorismo de la nada." *Buenos Aires Literaria,* no. 9 (June 1953): 25–38.

Bartholomew, Roy, ed. *Cien poesías rioplatenses* (anthology). Comment on "Elena Bellamuerte." Buenos Aires: Raigal, 1954.

Becco, Horacio J. "Bibliografía de Macedonio Fernández." *Buenos Aires Literaria,* no. 9 (June 1953).

Bersani, Leo. *Balzac to Beckett: Center and Circumference in French Fiction.* New York: Oxford University Press, 1970.

Borges, Jorge Luis. Address delivered at the funeral of Macedonio Fernández. *Sur.* no. 209–10 (1952) : 145–47.

—— ed. *Macedonio Fernández* (anthology). Buenos Aires: Ediciones Culturales Argentinas, 1961.

Borges, Jorge Luis and Norman Thomas di Giovanni. "Autobiographical Notes." *New Yorker,* September 19, 1970, pp. 40–99.

Borinsky de Risler, Alicia. *"Humorística, novelística y obra abierta en Macedonio Fernández."* Ph.D dissertation, University of Pittsburgh, 1971.

——. "Macedonio: su proyecto novelístico." *Hispamérica,* no. 1 (1972): 31–48.

——. *Macedonio y sus otros.* Buenos Aires: Ediciones Corregidor, 1975.

Burke, Kenneth. *Counter-Statement.* Berkeley and Los Angeles: University of California Press, 1968.

Campbell, Joseph, ed. *Myths, Dreams and Religion.* New York: E. P. Dutton, 1970.

Cortázar, Julio. *Rayuela.* Buenos Aires: Editorial Sudamericana, 1968.

Fernández Latour, Enrique. Address delivered at the funeral of Macedonio Fernández. *Sur,* no. 209–10 (1952): 148.

I

————. "Un episodio epistolar entre Juan B. Justo y Macedonio
Fernández." *La Nación,* February 5, 1956.

————. "Macedonio Fernández, candidato a Presidente." *La
Prensa,* January 9, 1966.

Fernández Moreno, César. *Introducción a Macedonio Fernández.*
Buenos Aires: Talia, 1960.

Forster, E. M. *Aspects of the Novel.* New York: Harcourt, Brace
and World, 1927.

García, German Leopoldo, ed. *Hablan de Macedonio Fernández*
(eleven interviews). Buenos Aires: Carlos Pérez Editor,
1968.

Gide, André. *Les Faux-Monnayeurs.* Paris: Gallimard, 1925.

————. *Journal des Faux-Monnayeurs.* Paris: Gallimard, 1927.

Gómez de la Serna, Ramón. "Retrato de Macedonio Fernández."
In *Obras completas,* vol. 2. Barcelona: AHR, 1957.

Hume, David. *A Treatise of Human Nature.* Oxford: Clarendon
Press, 1964.

James, William. *The Principles of Psychology.* 1890; rpt. New
York: Dover, 1950.

————. *Varieties of Religious Experience.* New York: New American Library, 1958.

Jitrik, Noé. "Destrucción de formas en las narraciones." In
America Latina en su literatura, compiled by César
Fernández Moreno. Mexico: Siglo Veintiuno, 1972.

————. "La novela futura de Macedonio Fernández." In *Nueva
novela latinoamericana,* compiled by Jorge Lafforgue, pp.
30–70, Buenos Aires: Paidós, 1972.

Jurado, Alicia. "Aproximación a Macedonio Fernández."
    Ficción, no. 7 (May–June 1957): 65–78.

Mercier, Vivian. *The New Novel From Queneau to Pinget.* New
    York: Farrar, Straus and Giroux, 1971.

Obieta, Adolfo de. "Mi padre Macedonio Fernández." *Revista
    de la Universidad de la Plata,* no. 3, (1958): 147–50.

————. "Macedonio Fernández: Una mesa de diez metros y un
    día infinito." *La Opinión Cultural,* January 21, 1974, p. 9.

Pagés Larraya, Antonio. "Macedonio Fernández, un payador."
    Humanitas (Monterrey, Mexico), no. 3, (1962): 315–28.

Petit de Murat, Ulyses. "Jorge Luis Borges y la revolución
    literaria de *Martín Fierro.*" *Correo Literario,* January 1 and
    15, 1944.

Porcio, César. "Un viajero que no regresó del país del ensueño."
    La Nación, supplement, January 26, 1930, p. 39.

Robbe-Grillet, Alain. *Pour un nouveau roman.* Paris: Editions de
    Minuit, 1963.

Rodríguez Monegal, Emir. "Macedonio Fernández, Borges y el
    Ultraismo." *Número,* no. 19 (April–June 1952): 171–83.

Salvador, Nélida. "Macedonio Fernández y su poemática del
    pensar." *Comentario* (Buenos Aires) 11 (1964): 45–54.

Sarraute, Nathalie. *L'ére du soupçon.* Paris: Gallimard, 1956.

Schopenhauer, Arthur. *The World as Will and Representation.* 2
    vols. Translated by E. F. J. Payne. New York: Dover,
    1966.

Soler Cañas, Luis. "Algunos colaboradores de *El Tiempo.*"
    Clarín, August 3, 1958.

————. "Testimonios de un joven singular." *Clarín,* April 11, 1974.

Stace, Walter T. *The Teachings of the Mystics.* New York: New American Library, 1960.

Sterne, Lawrence. *The Life and Opinions of Tristram Shandy.* New York: Pocket Books, 1957.

Stevick, Philip, ed. *The Theory of the Novel.* New York: Free Press, 1967.

Sturrock, John. *The French New Novel: Claude Simon, Michel Butor, Alain Robbe-Grillet.* London: Oxford University Press, 1969.

Sypher, Wylie. *Rococo to Cubism in Art and Literature.* New York: Random House, 1960.

————. *Loss of Self in Modern Literature and Art.* New York: Random House, 1962.

Unamuno, Miguel de. "Pirandello y yo." In *Obras completas,* 2d. ed. Barcelona: Vergara, 1958. 10:544–48.

————. *Niebla.* Madrid: Espasa-Calpe, 1968.

Virasoro, Miguel A. Review of *No toda es vigilia la de los ojos abiertos. Síntesis* 2 (October 1928): 224–27.

Watt, Ian. *The Rise of the Novel: Studies in Defoe, Richardson, and Fielding.* Berkeley and Los Angeles: University of California Press, 1967.

Zaehner, R. C. *Mysticism Sacred and Profane.* London: Oxford University Press, 1967.

Zimmer, Heinrich. *Philosophies of India.* Edited by Joseph Campbell. Cleveland and New York: World Publishing Company, 1961.

Index

214

and Suffered Two Losses Every Day"), 52–53
Don Quixote, 147–148, 187, 188
dreams 88–91

"Elena Bellamuerte," 24–25
El Progreso, 6, 7
El Tiempo, 9
"El Zapallo que se hizo Cosmos" ("The Squash That Became the Cosmos"), 51

Fernández, Adolfo (brother of Macedonio), 10
Fernández, Macedonio: symbol of Argentinity, x; place in Argentine literature, xii–xv; disciples, xiv, 27–30; precursor of Ultraism, 17, 27, 28; and martinfierristas, 38–44; presidential candidacy, 41–43; principal works, 47–60; correspondence with William James, 20–22; attorney, 14–15; meets Borges, 26–27; metaphysics, 19–24; 61–94; theory of art, 97–100; theory of the novel, 97–135; theory of the literary character, 137–160; "Ningunamuno," 165; authorial intrusion, 190; and the President's novel, 193–196
Fernández Latour, Enrique, 12, 13, 30, 42–43
Fernández Moreno, César, 102–105
Flaubert, Gustave, 160
Ford, Ford Madox, 182

Forster, E.M., 177, 183
Fuentes, Carlos, xii

Gass, William, 173
Gide, André, 155, 160–161, 196–197
Gómez de la Serna, Ramón, xii, 28, 48, 109, 115, 196
González Lanuza, Eduardo, xiii, 29
Gris, Juan, 160
Güiraldes, Ricardo, 28, 30, 35

Hegel, G.W.F., 69
Hidalgo, Alberto, 29, 31, 49
Hobbes, Thomas, 90
Hume, David, 76–78, 87, 90
Husserl, Edmund, 168

Idealism, 73–78, 98, 100, 104, 105–106, 125–126; and language, 125–127; and literary characters, 137–146
Ingenieros, José, 9–10, 20

James, Henry, 177, 189, 190
James, William, 20–22, 75–79, 189
Jiménez, Juan Ramón, 25, 50
Jitrik, Noé, 1, 98–99, 110, 114–116, 121, 139, 142, 144, 158, 163
Journal des "Faux-Monnayeurs" (Journal of "The Counterfeiters"), 160, 196–197
Jurado, Alicia, 86–87
Justo, Juan B., 8, 9

Kant, Immanuel, 66, 68–69, 107, 151